DANIEL

Daniel

by

HARRY BELL

June 2002
Published by
GOSPEL TRACT PUBLICATIONS
7 Beech Avenue, Glasgow, G41 5BY, U.K.

Copyright © 1982
Gospel Tract Publications
ISBN 0 948417 80 3

First printing December 1982
Second printing June 2002

Printed by
GOSPEL TRACT PUBLICATIONS

Contents

Dedication	6
Explanatory	7
Introduction	9
Chapter 1	31
Chapter 2	47
Chapters 3 & 4	63
Chapters 5 & 6	81
Chapter 7	99
Chapter 8	115
Chapter 9	121
Chapters 10 - 12	139

Dedication

To Kate — Harry's Sister — She did what she could

Explanatory.

The substance of this book was given as a series of addresses at Plas Menai, North Wales, in 1959. The audience was predominantly young people who had come aside for one week to study the Word of God under this gifted teacher. The style reflects this fact in its admirable simplicity.

In seeking to put these talks into readable form, every effort has been made to maintain Mr. Bell's mode of delivery, and in effect the result is almost a verbatim report, eliminating only repetitions of emphasis, and anecdotes which would not now be appropriate.

It should perhaps be mentioned that Mr. Bell never used a single note, and all his scriptural references were given from memory.

Harry Bell of Jarrow was a man who suffered much in the body, and his sight in particular was a major handicap for one who read so avidly, but if there was any one thing which marked this dear saint of God it was his humility in the manner in which he carried his great gift, at the same time never complaining of his handicaps. He was a gracious man, full of compassion, yet a champion for truth. He loved God's Word, God's people and as to God's Beloved Son, His glory was the theme of his constant thought. How many times had he concluded his word of ministry by reciting or singing, "Far above all, far above all; God has exalted Him far above all". He reflected the Blessed Man that he loved.

T.W.Smith

Introduction.

The book of the prophet Daniel is a startling, an amazing book. Any schoolboy will tell you that since the days of the Assyrians there have been four world empires, and will no doubt tell you from history who those four were, but we do not need to look at history, for the Bible tells us here in the Book of Daniel of those four great powers, and history but confirms what the Word says. You will have read of Alexander the Great and his four generals Ptolemy, Lysimachus, Cassander and Seleucus, of Julius Caesar, Pompey, Scipio, and of Cleopatra of Egypt and Antiochus Epiphanes of Syria — all great historical characters; well they are all in this book of Daniel. Daniel depicted these great figures and told us who they would be, what they would do, how they would live and die, and *Daniel told of it all long before they existed.* Daniel prophesied the whole course of history, and not only that, but he even foretold when Christ would die, to the very year when our Lord would be crucified. He prophesied how long Israel would be in captivity, and when they would return, it is all in the Book of Daniel. Modernists, men who do not believe in the Bible, try to get rid of this, for Daniel's prophecy condemns them. Daniel's prophecy shows the inspiration of the Word, so they try to get rid of it by making out that Daniel lived much later, that he lived after all these events had taken place, so that he was not prophesying but simply telling about the past — but there is one thing that defeats the Modernists, absolutely confounds them — the prophet Ezekiel lived in those times, and he mentions Daniel twice. He would not have mentioned Daniel if Daniel had not existed, so we know that Daniel did exist when the Bible says he did. Furthermore, Daniel wrote of modern times, and the current

DANIEL

moral tendencies, inventions, etc. Further, we have the authority of our Lord for it, in Matthew 24, so then Daniel is a book of startling, wonderful and amazing prophecies. It will thrill us to think of these things, but then there is something far more than that, Daniel gives a wonderful picture of Christ; his book from end to end is filled with truth about God's beloved Son, the One who is to reign and have dominion throughout the Universe.

Mr. Bell read from Daniel chapter one.

The Book of Daniel as we all know is a prophetic book, it tells about things which are going to come to pass. When I say it is a prophetic book, of course, I should say that in the primary sense the whole Bible is prophetic — John 3:16 is a prophetic scripture. The word prophecy really means "the telling out of God's mind". Well, in that sense all the Bible is prophetic, but the book of Daniel is prophetic also in the second sense of the word, that is, it foretells the mind of God concerning the future. It is a prophetic book telling things to come, but not for the purpose of merely being interesting — it is very interesting to get to know what is going to happen — but the book of Daniel was not written simply for that, for it was written primarily with this end in view — to tell out the glories of the Lord, to enlighten us concerning those times to come when the Lord shall be universally glorified. So its message is not one of mere interest or fascination, but to direct our eyes towards the Lord Jesus Christ. Prophecy in the Bible is a most interesting and thrilling subject, but it is also an extensive subject and it covers a tremendous part of the Word of God. So for an understanding of the book of Daniel, we need to have some understanding of the Bible as a whole, otherwise we will not appreciate what Daniel, by the Spirit of God, is telling us. Having this in view I want to try and lay a foundation; I want to take you with me through all the ages of God's dealing right back into the past, then right

INTRODUCTION

on into the future, and to show how in every age God has been dealing with His creature man; to show that in all the ages there is a Divine purpose like a golden thread running through all those ages and God will work steadily onward until He has accomplished that purpose.

First of all, then, I want you to think with me of a "past eternity" before the universe came into being — when I say "past eternity" that is really a contradiction of terms; eternity can never pass, but you know that I am directing your minds back into the eternal past. Now what took place then? Well we do not know, but this, in the Gospel of John chapter 1, verse 1, we read "In the beginning was the Word, and the Word was with God, and the Word was God". Away back then in eternity, go as far back as ever you care to go, millions and millions and millions of years ago, eternally back, without beginning, and the Lord Jesus, God the Son, was with His Father God; He ever was with God. Also the Spirit of God is called in the epistle to the Hebrews, the Eternal Spirit, so that right back in eternity, going as far back as ever you care to go, there was the Father, the Son and the Spirit, the triune God, without beginning or end, from everlasting to everlasting.

Now can we tell of anything that happened in that bygone time before the creation of the world? We know very little, but God has revealed just a modicum of truth concerning this 'past eternity', and we know this, that in the mind of God you and I were in His eternal counsels, you and I were eternally in the thoughts of God. In the Epistle to Titus (and the opening chapter) Paul says "In hope of eternal life, which God, that cannot lie, promised before the world began" — now here is a consultation within the Trinity, a discussion between the Father, the Son and the Spirit, and before the world began it was planned in the Divine counsels, that you and I should have eternal life — "In hope of eternal life, which God, that cannot lie, promised before the world began". Again in I Peter 1 we read of our Lord Jesus Christ:

12 DANIEL

"The Lamb of God, Who was foreordained before the foundation of the world, but was manifest in these last times for you" — the Lord Jesus Christ, then, eternally, before the world was, was set apart, the Lamb of God to die for you and me. Yet again, in Ephesians 1 we read, "God hath blessed us with all spiritual blessings in heavenly places, according as He chose us in Him before the foundation of the world". So then, back in what we call "an eternity past" the Triune God was there and there was consultation within that Triune Godhead, and they purposed that you and I would have life, that the the Lord Jesus Christ would die as the Lamb of God and that you and I would be blessed with all spiritual blessings in heavenly places.

Before Thy hands had made the sun to rule the day,
Or earth's foundation laid, or fashioned Adam's clay,
What thoughts of peace and mercy flowed
In Thy great heart of love, Oh God.

Now, does the Scripture tell us of anything else which took place in that time? Yes. In Isaiah 14 and Ezekiel chapter 28 we read that there was a revolt in heaven. Isaiah says "How art thou fallen from heaven, O Lucifer, son of the morning. . . thou saidst in thine heart, I will ascend into heaven, I will exalt my throne above the stars of God . . . Yet thou shalt be brought down to hell, to the sides of the pit". Or again, in Ezekiel 28, addressing Satan in the figure of the King of Tyre, God says (v.14) that he was "anointed cherub that covereth . . . Thou wast in Eden the garden of God, every precious stone was thy covering" ; then both Isaiah and Ezekiel tell how he was "perfect in all his ways, till iniquity was found in him". Away then before the worlds were, there was a revolt in heaven — Satan and his angels revolting against God. In Matthew 12 the devil is called "the prince of the demons" for he led those of his fellow-conspirators, the angels that fell with him, against the throne of God. In I

INTRODUCTION 13

Timothy 3 and verse 6, Paul, speaking of the elders, says "not a novice, lest being lifted up with pride he fall into condemnation (error) of the devil" — the devil's error was that he thought to exalt himself above the stars of God and for that he fell and lost his position as being the "anointed cherub that covereth". It would seem, fellow believers, that Satan before he fell was the leader of the heavenly praises, because in Isaiah 14 and Ezekiel 28 we read of all the musical instruments connected with him — pipes, tabrets, etc., etc. — so it would seem that as the anointed cherub he led the praises to God, but now, that place (as man), that place (in His manhood) belongs to our Lord Jesus Christ, as it says in Hebrews 2 "in the midst of the Church will I sing praise unto God", so our Lord Jesus, as man, is the leader of God's people in their praise to God.

We come to that point when God created the heavens and the earth. It says in Genesis 1:1 "In the beginning God created the heaven and the earth". How long ago that was we do not know. Scientists tell us about millions and millions of years. Well, they can talk about as many millions as they like and we would not dispute them in the least. It may well be that this earth is millions of years old, and if scientists "put all these noughts on" that does not worry us in the least. We have no reason for doubting that God could have made the heaven and the earth millions and millions of years ago, if He chose to do so. When He made it we do not know. So, God made the heaven and the earth, and then we find a great catastrophe, a great calamity comes in, and we read in Genesis 1:2 "and the earth was without form and void". Waste and void; and "darkness was upon the face of the deep, and the Spirit of God moved on the waters". Now here is the calamity. God made the heaven and the earth, but there is the earth wholly under water, waste and void, and darkness on the face of the deep. The earth was there, for when God began to work the third day it says "let the waters be gathered together into one place . . . and let the dry land

DANIEL

appear". So on the third day He brought the dry land out of the waters (it was already there; it had been for a long time); on the third day He brought it out from the waters. In Isaiah 43 Isaiah says God did not make the world without form and void; it became like that in Genesis 1:2. What happened we do not know; what calamity had come in we cannot say; it may have been the fall of Satan and his hosts that resulted in the ruin of the earth, but whether that be so or not, there it is, a calamity has come in, a cataclysm, and the earth is without form and void and darkness was upon the face of the deep. Now God starts again, and in six days He makes heaven and earth. He brings the earth out of the water, separates the vapour which surrounds it, and makes the firmament appear. On the sixth day as the triumph of His handiwork God makes man (in I Corinthians 15 he is called the first man, Adam). So God starts with His fresh creation and He makes man, He makes Adam, and He says of Adam "Let us make man in our own image and in our likeness". Thus God has made a perfect world, clothed it with grass and flowers, trees and shrubs, etc., and fills the world with animals, birds, fishes and so forth, and above it all He places man—"And God gave Adam dominion". The Word says that Adam had dominion over every living thing; Adam could say to a lion "Come here" and it would come; he could say to a bear "Go yonder" and it would go; he could call a fish out of the sea. God gave Adam dominion over everything in creation. Psalm 8 says "Thou hast set him over the work of Thine hand" and so Adam was made in the likeness of God, a little lower than the angels, and he had dominion over all God's creation, and Adam gave names to all God's creatures.

How long that period lasted in the Garden of Eden I cannot tell. Somehow I think that it did not last very long, but I do not know. There was Adam in the garden with his wife, Eve. God had placed him there in all that beautiful serenity, and they were so completely one that in Genesis 5 it is said "He called *their* name Adam; and there they were in

INTRODUCTION   15

innocence in the Garden of Eden. But sin came in, the tempter appeared; Satan himself in the form of a serpent, and you know how he tempted Adam and Eve. By the way, men in the world scoff the Bible story of the fall of Adam, the serpent speaking and so forth—but there is one interesting fact; the Hebrew word for serpent is the word which we use in English for boa constrictor— perhaps sometimes in zoological gardens you may have seen one, that tremendous snake-like creature, the boa constrictor. Now the remarkable thing is this: the boa constrictor is the only animal with a boney structure which crawls along the ground— showing that it was never originally intended to do so, but because of the fall, because of the serpent's tempting of Adam and Eve, God said dust would be the serpent's meat and on its belly would it go, because of its onslaught against the creature of God.

When Adam and Eve fell their fall had a result spiritually, morally and bodily. *Spiritually*— "In the day thou eatest thereof thou shalt surely die", and Adam was cast out of the garden, he died spiritually; he was separated from God. *Morally*— before Adam sinned, he did not know good or evil. If you had talked to Adam about stealing or telling lies or about unkindness, he would not have known what you were talking about. Adam had not the knowledge of sin and evil. He knew no such thing as sin. He was an innocent man with no such knowledge as that of good and evil, but when he disobeyed God he partook of that forbidden fruit, the tree of the knowledge of good and evil, and Adam got a knowledge of sin, and he and Eve looked upon themselves and saw themselves as horrible, naked, exposed sinners. He had now got what he never had before—a knowledge of sin. He fell *spiritually,* he was separated from God; he fell *morally,* he got a knowledge of sin; then he fell *bodily*— God said "Of dust thou wast and unto dust shalt thou return". If Adam had not sinned he would have been alive now, in the body, but because of his sin, "to dust shalt thou return". The first

16   DANIEL

dispensation of man then is the DISPENSATION of INNOCENCE, in Eden, when Adam and Eve lived there in all the untramelled purity of the garden.

Now from the fall there enters in the DISPENSATION of CONSCIENCE— Adam has passed out of the presence of God. What has he got to help him and guide him — he has a conscience. If we read in Romans 1 about those days it says three times "God gave them up" —God gave up men because of their sin. But in Romans 2 it speaks of conscience; it speaks of men having the works of the law written in their hearts, their conscience also bearing witness. God gave to Adam and Eve a conscience. The moment Adam sinned he had a conscience. He looked upon himself. He saw himself naked, and he fled from the presence of God. He had a conscience of sin. The word conscience comes from two words — "con" meaning "together" and "science" which is "knowledge"—so conscience = knowledge together; that is, knowledge that we hold in common with God. Man has a moral sense of right and wrong, and that is conscience, a knowledge he holds in common with God. That dispensation of conscience began with the fall of Adam, and it goes on until the time of the flood, and if you look in Genesis 4 you will find there is a line of men—Cain, Lamech, etc.—and they are all wicked men. They are inventing the harp and organ; they are discovering brass and iron; they learn the making of tents and so on. That is the line of Genesis 4. But in Genesis 5 there is another line, the line of Seth, and he is "the son of God". It reads "and then began men to call upon the name of the Lord". So the age of conscience started with the fall of Adam and it issued into two lines of descent—Cain's line and Seth's line. Cain's line discovering things down here on earth; Seth's line discovering the things of God.

Now that condition of things went on until the flood. Then men having gone worse and worse, God said He could no

INTRODUCTION 17

longer go on with man; so He allowed them a further 120 years. And in those 120 years Noah preached righteousness, and at the end of that period the flood came, and only eight of them (Noah and his wife, his three sons and their wives) were saved out of the flood. The flood came and destroyed that world, and makes a break here. The apostle Peter in his 2nd Epistle, speaking of before the flood says "the world that then was". Again he uses the expression "if God spared not the *old* world"; so the world before the flood was the world that "then was" —it was the "old world". Here is God making a dispensational break, bringing a new age into being at the end of the flood. So Noah comes out of the ark and there begins the third dispensation.

We have had the dispensation of innocence, the dispensation of conscience, and now the dispensation of HUMAN GOVERNMENT. God indicated to Noah that He was to put human government in his hands, and says "I will put the dread of you on all cattle". Now you will note that is very different from Adam, for Adam could call the animals of the earth and they would come to him—they were all subject to him. Noah had not that power, but God said to Noah "I will put the dread of you on all cattle", and it is true today, the beasts have a fear of mankind. Then He told Noah He would put a change in his diet—"every clean animal and bird was given to him for food". But up to the flood man had been vegetarian, for "God gave Adam every green herb to feed upon". So there is a change of status; a change of food; and there is a change of government. God tells Noah He is going to put government in his hands—"and whoso sheddeth man's blood, by man shall his blood he shed". That had never been said before, it had not been said to Adam or Abel; so comes into the hands of man the responsibility of human government.

At this point perhaps we may pause, and ask, Why is God dealing in these different ways? Innocence, Conscience,

18   DANIEL

Human Government; what is God's purpose? Man has fallen, and God is trying him under every circumstance, in every possible way to see if man will obey Him, and praise and glorify Him, so He brings in all these different ways of dealing.

The age of human government reached its climax, its height, with the Tower of Babel. There in Genesis chapter 11 they said "Go to, let us build us a city, a tower . . . and let us make us a name", and they built this great tower in rebellion against God. The previous chapter says they were led by Nimrod the mighty hunter, Nimrod the Cushite, the black man or the mighty hunter, and they were led by him in this revolt against God. God had said there would not be a flood any more. Ah, but they said we will protect ourselves, we will not trust God, we will build a city, a tower, lest we be scattered upon the earth. Thus they showed ignorance of God, ignorance of heaven, and ignorance of themselves. Ignorance of God in that they said "lest we be scattered upon the earth" on which God had promised He would not scatter them; God had promised He would not send a flood. Ignorance of heaven; they said "Let us build a tower whose top shall reach to heaven". They did not realise that they could not get to heaven by any works of their own. Ignorance of themselves; it says "they had brick for stone", brick of their own make, instead of stone, God's provision. And they had slime for mortar—typical of their own works. Such is man's utter rebellion against God.

In chapter 12 begins the new age, the PATRIARCHAL DISPENSATION, of Abram and his family. In Genesis 12 God calls Abram out saying "Get thee out of thy country and from thy kindred and from thy father's house, unto a land that I will shew thee . . . and I will make thy name great . . . and I will make thee a blessing [God promises seven things there by the way] and in thee shall all families of the earth be blessed". You will have noted that the men of Shinar who

INTRODUCTION 19

built the tower said "Let *us* make us a name", but God says to Abram "You come with me and *I* will make you a name" ("I will make thy name great"). They tried to make their own name, but God says to Abram "I will make thee a name".

Now begins the patriarchal age—Abram, Isaac, Jacob, Joseph and the fathers of Israel down in Egypt. This period lasted for 400 years. Listen, fellow believers, what was the character of that age? Just this, they had no home on earth—God called Abraham into Canaan, and he did not own a foot of it. God said "Walk up and down in the land", and he was a stranger. God said to him that He would give him the land, but for the present he would be a stranger and pilgrim in it. You may ask why that was; why would God have Abraham a stranger in the land He was to give him? In Genesis 15 God tells Abraham "The iniquity of the Amorites is not yet full" —God had been suffering the wickedness of this people for centuries; but their "iniquity was not yet full" so God did not feel it was the time to drive them out. By and by He would drive them out, because of their wickedness, but meantime Abram was not to possess the land for 400 years. At the end of that four centuries when the iniquity of the Amorites was full, God would call the children of Israel out of Egypt and bring them into Canaan.

In the patriarchal age we have four outstanding men: Abraham the man of *faith*. It says in Genesis 15 "Abraham believed God and it was accounted to him for righteousness". Isaac the man of *love*. The first mention of love in the Bible is in connection with Isaac, and three times over in Isaac's life we read of the word "love". Jacob the man of *hope*. Jacob goes over the brook Jabbok and he has only a staff in his hand; he has nothing else at all, no home, no shelter, no friends, but God says "Jacob, I will guide you all the way, and I will bring you back into your own land and I will enrich you and multiply you", and for twenty years the vision of hope burns brightly in Jacob's mind, until after those long years his hopes are fulfilled. Abraham the man of

20   DANIEL

faith, Isaac the man of love, Jacob the man of hope. And so Joseph comes in, and in Joseph we find all those three things—the faith of Abraham, the love of Isaac and the hope of Jacob. Joseph's life is divided into three sections—Joseph with his parents; Joseph in the pit and the prison; Joseph in the palace. Joseph with his parents was the man of faith. God gave him two visions showing him that he would be the ruler over his brethren, and Joseph believed God. Joseph in the pit and in the prison was the man of hope; he hoped for the day when God would deliver him. But Joseph in the palace was the man of love. His rascally, cut-throat brethren came, and he forgave the lot of them, and richly met their needs, and blessed them superabundantly—the man of love on the throne. He is the man of faith with his parents, the man of hope in the prison, and he is the man of love in the palace.

So we come to the age of law. God brought Israel out of Egypt after 400 years and God brought them into the Wilderness. In Exodus chapter 19 God prepares to give them His law. Now this DISPENSATION of the LAW lasted for 1,400 years, and I want you to think with me of the character of it. For 1,400 years God had an earthly people, a nation on the earth. For 1,400 years you could have gone to a certain geographical spot, a definite place on the earth, and you could have said "The people of God are here; this is God's place; this is God's earthly people"—that place was the land of Canaan. In Deuteronomy chapter 7 verse 6 God says He has chosen them to be a special people unto Himself, above all nations that are on the face of the earth. So then, here is a "special people" whom God owns, on the earth; an earthly nation belonging to God. In Joshua chapter 4 when the ark is going over Jordan, God tells Joshua to erect stones—"that all the earth may know". Here is a testimony to God on earth. In Amos chapter 3 verse 2 God says to Israel "You only have I known of all families upon the earth, therefore I will punish you". Thus the dispensation of the law ushers in

INTRODUCTION

an earthly nation; a people on earth whom God owned as His own.

Now why did God give them a law? It was for two reasons, (1) Conviction; (2) Construction. *First God gave them a law to teach them that they were sinners.* Moses said in Exodus 19 when God was giving the law, "God is come here to prove you". He gave the law to prove them, to show that they were sinners. Romans chapter 3 says "By the law is the knowledge of sin". God gave the law to teach Israel that they were sinners. In 1st Timothy chapter 1 Paul tells us that the law was given to lawless ones. It was given to criminals and sinners to prove that they were guilty before God. The law was given to Israel to show that they were sinners, to give them knowledge of guilt, so that when Christ came, knowing that they were sinners, they would turn to Him in repentance, seek forgiveness, seek the pardon of the cross of Calvary. But then *the law had another purpose.* It is called in Ephesians chapter 2 "the middle wall of partition" — God put a fence around Israel, a wall, to wall them off from the other nations, to wall them off as His own, and that wall was the law, the middle wall of partition bracketing Israel off from the Gentiles, fencing off Israel as being the people of God. Now you know, beloved, that that law is given by God in love. Deuteronomy 33 says "From His right hand went a fiery law. Yea He loved the people". It was a fiery law, it tried Israel, it tested them, it searched them, it involved trouble. Ah, but it was given in love; there was love behind it, the love of God, for it was all intended to show them they were sinners, with a view to bringing them to Christ.

Now the dispensation of the law can be divided into three sections, in this way: (1) we have Israel without a king: (2) Israel with a king; (3) Israel under another king. What I mean is this: In the book of Joshua, Judges and the early chapters of I Samuel (up to chapter 9) Israel were in the land without a king, God was their king, but then in I Samuel 9 they lust after a king like the Gentiles. Well, God gave them a

22 DANIEL

king, and that condition of things lasted right through 1st and 2nd Samuel, 1st and 2nd Kings, 1st and 2nd Chronicles, then at the end of 2nd Chronicles their king is taken from them and they get another king, and from that day onwards Israel has always been under another king; they have always been under the yoke of the Gentiles. At the end of 2nd Chronicles Nebuchadnezzar comes in and captures them and takes them off to Babylon, so they came under another—a foreign—king. Since then they have always been under a foreign yoke and they are today. So we trace Israel's three stages under the law — without a king, with a king and under the rule of another king (through Ezra, Nehemiah, Esther and right until the time when the Lord sets aside His earthly people in the cross of Christ—when Christ died for sinners).

Well now, the dispensation of the law ended with the cross of Christ. Scripture is most definite about that. Hebrews says "Once in the end of the age hath He appeared to put away sin by the sacrifice of Himself". In Galatians we read "The law was our schoolmaster to bring us to Christ", or literally "The law was our schoolmaster up to Christ". The law was intended to last until Christ came and died, and then it was the end of the law. So, then, *the dispensation of the law ended with Christ crucified.*

Now God has brought in another dispensation — and what dispensation is that? It is the DISPENSATION of GRACE; the dispensation of the grace of God. Now what characterises this age? Well first it is the climax of all ages, the summit of them all. We read in I Corinthians chapter 10 "All these things happened unto them for examples, and were written for our admonition upon whom the ends of the world (literally 'of the ages') are come". Now, all dispensations then are finished. This is the summum bonum, this is the apex, the goal of all dispensations, it is the crowning point of God's purposes. There never was an age

INTRODUCTION 23

like this and (on the earth) there never will be — it is the height, the peak of all ages. You know, it has troubled some of God's children, as to how it is that there will be sacrifices on the earth when the Church is gone. They feel that is going backwards—of course it is going backwards, because this is the climax, the crown of all dispensations, so the dispensations after it can only go backward, they cannot go forward. Well now, what makes this age such a distinct, such a crowning dispensation, high above all others? We have had Innocence, Conscience, Human Government, the Patriarchal age, the Law, but now we have come to the greatest age which stands out among them all. What makes it so different?

Well (see Luke24). "Thus it was written, and thus it behoved Christ to suffer and to rise from the dead . . . *that repentance and remission of sins might be preached in His name among all nations"*. Beloved, that never happened before. We are living in an age when through the death and resurrection of Christ "repentance and remission of sins are being preached among all nations" — all may live, for Christ has died. That is something which was never heard before. Again, in Colossians chapter 1 we read of "the mystery which hath been hid from the ages and generations" (but now is made manifest) which is *"Christ in you the hope of glory"*. Now the word "mystery" means "secret". Colossians speaks then of a secret which was hidden from all the other ages, and it is "Christ in you the hope of glory". Today, God is gathering out a people from the Gentiles, a people saved by precious blood, saved by the grace of God, and Christ dwells in them, and He is the hope of Heavenly glory. Now you can read the Old Testament through, and you will never read anything like that— of the gathering in of the Gentiles, of Christ dwelling within them—(in them) the hope of glory, heavenly glory. It is something of which the Old Testament speaks absolutely nothing. The Old Testament speaks of blessing to the Gentiles; oh yes, but it is always inferior to

24   DANIEL

Israel; it is "rejoice ye Gentiles with His people". There is joy for the Gentiles but the Jews in particular are God's people. But here is something to be where Jew and Gentile are alike, where "in Christ there is neither Jew nor Greek, Barbarian, Scythian, bond nor free, but Christ is all and in all".

Then thirdly, fellow believers, this dispensation is above all other dispensations because God promises to you and me *blessings that the Old Testament saints never had* nor ever will have. Hebrews chapter 11 says "These all died in faith"—Abraham, Isaac and Jacob and so on—"not having received the promises, but having seen them afar off". "God having provided some better thing for us in that they without us should not be made perfect". Beloved, God has provided "some better thing" for you, and me, that Adam never knew, nor Abraham nor Isaac nor Jacob nor Joseph nor David — He has provided "some better thing". You and I, child of God, are going to be the aristocracy of Heaven, the very apex of the purposes of God; God gives blessings to you and me far above any order of His creatures. We read in Ephesians chapter 1 "God hath blessed us with all spiritual blessings in heavenly places in Christ Jesus". He never says that of Abraham, Isaac, Jacob, etc. It is something reserved distinctly and specially for His own. Our Lord said of John the Baptist "Of all them that had risen aforetime there had not risen a greater than John the Baptist, but nevertheless (He says) he that is least in the Kingdom of Heaven is greater than he". The very least in the Kingdom of Heaven is greater than John the Baptist. You and I have a position of dignity and blessing and riches of glory far beyond the Old Testament saints.

Now exactly what characterises this age? Well James says (Acts 15) "God has visited the Gentiles to take out of them a pepple for His name". You remember that under law God had an earthly people; He has none now. God had an earthly nation; He has none now. God is gathering out of the nations

INTRODUCTION 25

a people for His name. Our Lord said (in John 17) that we are "not of this world" even as He is not of it. I will never forget many years ago hearing the late Mr. C.F. Hogg making a statement—it startled me at the time—but the more I live the more I can see the truth of it. Mr. Hogg said "If ever I pick up a book or a pamphlet and I read in that book or pamphlet about the Church on earth I say to myself there is no light here—no light here—there is no such thing as the Church on earth". It is true—the Church is a Heavenly Church linked with a Heavenly Man in the glory, identified with Christ for ever, and so our Lord says "They are not of this world, even as I am not of it". Ephesians chapter 1 says "Christ is set at God's own right hand in the heavenly places, and became Head over all things to the Church, which is His body". The Church is linked with the Heavenly Man in the Glory—the Lord Jesus Christ. There is the church locally, of course, there is the church at Llanfairfechan, at Heswall, at Barrow, or Jarrow where I live (the church locally), but there is no such thing as the Church on earth. The Church is linked with the Heavenly Man in the Glory Who is taking out of the Gentiles a people for His name.

Now just before we pass on, fellow believers, let me say concerning the Church there are *two* outstanding characteristics of this present age. We have God on earth, and we have a man in the Glory—something which does not belong to any former age, but it belongs to this age. *God on earth.* The Lord said "If I go not, the Comforter will not come, but if I go I will send Him unto you". God the Holy Spirit is dwelling on earth, and God has a redeemed people in whom the Spirit of God dwells, and He says "Ye are the temple of God". The Holy Spirit came down at Pentecost, and He has been down here ever since, and He will be down here until we are caught up—so we have got God dwelling on earth. Then secondly there is *the Man in the Glory.* The Word says our Lord (as man) ascended up and He sat down on the right hand of God. The scripture says He entered (He

26

DANIEL

passed through) the heavens, the scripture says He went far above all heavens. There is a pre-eminent Man at God's right hand—a Man who bears the scars of Calvary, and the thorn marks upon His brow, a Man with a riven side—crowned above all; and as I look at that man I see what God thinks of me. God says I am in Christ. God sees me in the person of His risen Son. Well, He has taken Christ, and He has placed Him far above all, and that is where He has placed me. You and I are seated in the heavenly places in Christ Jesus. You and I, then, have God on earth—and a man in the Glory.

Now look, beloved, for fourteen hundred years God had Israel with a temple, with sacrifices, with offerings, with ritual and so on — now, there are none of these things. Hebrews 12 says "We have not come unto the mount which might be touched" — that is, God does not deal with us through the senses; He does not deal with us by things which we can touch and handle. We have not material sacrifices or a material altar, we have none of these things. We live in the age of the Spirit, where God communicates and helps us by the Spirit (Paul says "If we have known Christ after the flesh from henceforth know we Him no more" —we know Him now not by the flesh, but by the Spirit, through faith in the Lord Jesus Christ) and the only two things that God has given us of a material character are the two ordinances of this age—baptism and the breaking of bread. Baptism, which speaks of our death in Christ, and the breaking of bread which speaks of Christ's death for us. The breaking of bread—the Lord's last command before He died; baptism—the Lord's last command before He ascended; the only two things of a material character which God has given to us.

Someone has said, and that truly, that it is so easy to practise Christianity. All that you need is a Bible, some bread, a bottle and a bath. A Bible, God's precious Word; some bread to remember the Lord; a bottle, the bottle of wine which we pour into the cup on the Lord's Day, and a

INTRODUCTION 27

bath big enough to baptise people in. Of course when I say a bath it has to be rather a big bath, for both the baptiser and the baptised go down into the water. It says in Acts 8 "they went down both into the water and he baptised him there".

So then, what comes after this age. *The Lord is coming* – and He might come at any moment. He said "if I go I will come again and receive you unto myself", and He is going to take us to the Father's house to be "forever with the Lord". And what then? Well, in Jeremiah 30 we read of a time of Jacob's trouble, when the nation of Israel will pass through a time of terrible trouble. Jeremiah says "I see every man with his hands upon his loins", "Alas for that day . . . that none is like it" "it is even the time of Jacob's trouble, but he shall be saved out of it". Or see Matthew 24, "There shall be a time of great tribulation such as never was in this world", and Revelation 3 says "Because thou hast kept the word of my patience, I also will keep thee from the hour of temptation (trial) that is to come upon all the world to try them that are on the earth". After the Church has gone, then, there is to come a time of great tribulation — it is *for Israel* and it is *for the world*. "But how do you know," says somebody, "that the Church will go home before that tribulation commences?" Well, I know it *because God says it!* God says it in language as plain as John 3:16 — that the Church *will not,* and *cannot* pass through the tribulation. Our brother read this morning in Revelation 5, there you have got the Church in Glory. The four living creatures and the four and twenty elders are *there*, with the Lord, and the tribulation does not start until the next chapter, chapter 6. So the Church is home then, before the tribulation begins. Now look, friends, you can look through Revelation from chapter 6 to chapter 18 and read all about the tribulation, and you will never read of the Church in it. Men put the Church there; God does not. God says the Church is not in it, but home—forever with the Lord. Beloved, forgive me for being

DANIEL

so dogmatic about this, but I long to see Christians brought into the light of God's word.

Someone may say "What about Matthew 24. But the Church has no connection with Matthew 24; it is never mentioned. The Lord said the temple would be destroyed. What has the Church got to do with the temple? The Lord distinctly said "Let them which are in Judea flee to the wilderness", and the Lord said they would see the Son of Man coming and they would mourn because of Him—but when my Lord comes I am not going to mourn, I am going to rejoice (Amen!). Oh, child of God, how clear, how gloriously clear is the word of God if only we take it in its beautiful simplicity.

Well, after the Church has gone there will be that seven year period of tribulation. In that day they will cry for vengeance (You and I do not want vengeance, it is the age of grace). In that day there are two peoples, there are 144,000 out of Israel and a multitude out of the Gentiles—but today Jew and Gentile are one. In that day they have got a temple, but today you and I are God's temple. So then clearly the present age must pass before the tribulation commences. The tribulation ends with the Lord coming back with His saints—in Revelation 19 He appears with the armies of heaven following Him, then in Revelation 20 He reigns for a thousand years, and you and I are going to reign for a thousand years, with the Lord, over the earth. Revelation 21 from verse 9 onwards describes that day—the Lord reigns from above, the city of Jerusalem is in the air, but in touch with the earth, and the kings of the earth bring their glory to the Lord, and the Lord rules completely for a thousand years—and if you want to know what it is like turn to Isaiah chapter eleven. The animals will lose their wildness; the wolf will lie down with the Lamb, the cockatrice will lose its poison—"they will not hurt or destroy in all my holy mountain and the earth will bring forth its fruits to the full, and the earth will be filled with the knowledge of the Lord as

INTRODUCTION 29

the waters cover the sea" (Isaiah 11), and in Zechariah 8 we find that death will be held in abeyance, for it says that old men will lean on their staffs for very age. Undertakers will go out of business in that long thousand years of millenial reign — sin will be held in control, and Christ will reign. Then at the end of the thousand years there will be Satan's last revolt (Revelation 20). He will be loosed for a little and will gather the nations together, and, after a thousand years of God's blessing, they will hurl themselves at Jerusalem, and God will destroy them. Then after that there will be the judgment of the Great White Throne.

Then (see Revelation 21 vs. 1-8) heaven and earth will pass away, and there will be a new heaven and a new earth, and Peter says (II Peter 3) in that new heaven and new earth righteousness will dwell, and in the whole universe God's glory will be manifested. Philippians chapter 2 tells us that just before that new heaven and new earth Christ will be acknowledged as Lord in heaven, earth and hell—the heaven above, the earth around and the depths beneath—celestial, terrestial, infernal—every knee shall bow and every tongue confess that Jesus Christ is Lord to the glory of God the Father. When this new heaven and new earth will come; you and I will be in heaven for ever with the Lord. Israel will be the centre of the new earth and the nations of the earth will be blessed under the beneficent, kindly reign of God through His blessed Son, the Lord Jesus Christ, and Ephesians chapter 3 says that "to God there will be glory in the Church through all eternity" and the Church for ever and ever will be the vehicle of God's glory — "unto Him be glory in the Church through all ages, world without end. Amen".

Well now, beloved, we have seen the ages of mankind, the dispensations; first the dispensation of innocence that ended in Eden, second the dispensation of conscience that ended with the flood, third the dispensation of human government that ended with the call of Abraham, then we read the patriarchal age ended with the exodus from Egypt, then the

DANIEL

age of the Law lasting for fourteen hundred years until the Lord comes, then we have the present age of grace, then when the Church has gone home there will be the Great Tribulation lasting for seven years, then the thousand years of the Lord's millenial reign, then the last revolt, and the new heaven and the new earth. Now, beloved, God is working with a purpose through all the ages—to one end—the glory of His Son.

> *And He shall have dominion*
> *O'er ocean, sea or shore,*
> *Far as the eagle's pinion*
> *Or dove's bright wings shall soar.*

We have tried in these things, fellow believers, to sketch the outline of the purposes of God, and we trust that the little groundwork which we have tried to lay may be a help to the young ones—especially to the young ones, but to us all, in the understanding of the further truth which we hope the Lord will bring before us.

Daniel Chapter One

Mr. Bell read Daniel Chapter one.

Before we look at the particular chapter that is before us I would like to try to say something about the character of the book of the prophet Daniel as a whole.

In the Old Testament there are four outstanding prophets—Isaiah, Jeremiah, Ezekiel, Daniel— I mean four outstanding prophets in the length of their prophecies, their books are larger than the other prophetic books of the Old Testament; they are commonly referred to as the major prophets. This is not to say they are more inspired than the other prophets, all Old Testament prophecy is equally inspired, but these books are larger, more lengthy, than the other writers—Joel, Amos and so forth, and they form the basis for Old Testament prophecy. There are five of these books then, commonly known as the major prophets, Isaiah, Jeremiah, Lamentations, Ezekiel and Daniel. Well now, Isaiah speaks of a lost revelation, Isaiah was told (in chapter 6) to shut the peoples' eyes, that they might not see, because of their sin and because of their rejection of God's truth; the revelation of God was taken from them, God gave them up to judicial blindness. Thus Isaiah speaks of a lost revelation. Jeremiah speaks of a lost joy. Jeremiah said, the people have committed two sins, "they have forsaken Me the fountain of living waters and have hewn out for themselves broken cisterns that could hold no water." Daniel speaks of a lost kingdom; Belshazzar the king came in and destroyed the kingdom of Israel and took away captives into Babylon; they lost their kingdom. Ezekiel speaks of a lost glory. Ezekiel in chapter 11, looks at the glory rising up from the temple and going out to the Mount of Olives and then returning into

32 DANIEL

Heaven and the glory of God was lost to Israel. Isaiah, then, speaks of a lost revelation, Jeremiah of a lost joy, Daniel of a lost kingdom and Ezekiel of a lost glory.

Daniel—his name means my God is judge—and Daniel's message, in keeping with his name; spoke of the judgment of God in relation to Israel. The object of Daniel's prophecy was this; God had always promised that Israel would be the chief nation on the earth, they would be the centre of God's Kingdom, and from them the blessings of God would issue out to all the earth, but now they had sinned and rebelled, and in II Kings 17, ten of the tribes were taken away captive into Assyria, and they never returned. Now in the end of the book of Chronicles the remaining two tribes with a remnant from the other tribes were taken away into Babylon, and the kingdom was gone. Now, what becomes of the promises of God? God had said Israel would be the chief nation on earth, but their land is wasted, the temple is destroyed, the people are in captivity—what is to become now of the promises of God? Furthermore, instead of Israel becoming the chief nation on earth, that privilege has passed to the Gentiles and we have the great world empire of Babylon instead of Israel. So the question would arise, what is God's purpose now? He has scattered His Kingdom, He has destroyed their nation, He has given dominion and power and world wide government into the hands of the Gentiles—well, what does God intend to do now?

The book of Daniel answers that question. It tells of what God intended to do, the purposes of God when He allowed the kingdom of Israel to be destroyed. The book of Daniel corresponds in a very striking way with the book of the Revelation. It deals with a people in captivity, a people who had got far away from God—it starts like that, and the book of the Revelation starts the same way. In the book of the Revelation, John addresses seven churches, Ephesus, Smyrna, Pergamos, Thyatira, Sardis, Philadelphia and Laodicea, and there is a measure of ruin in them all, a

CHAPTER 1

measure of departure and failure in all of them. So, Daniel starts with a failing people; John with failing churches. Then Daniel deals with four world empires, so does the book of the Revelation (cf Revelation 13:2 with Daniel chapter 7 where we have the same beasts mentioned, namely a lion, a bear, a leopard, and a fourth monstrous beast). In Revelation 13, we find the identical four world empires with which Daniel deals. Then Daniel shows the vision of the Lord upon the throne in Daniel chapter 7, and so we have in the book of the Revelation the Lord on the throne of glory. Then in Daniel (chapter 9 for instance) we have the great tribulation which shall come when the church is no longer here; so does the book of the Revelation. Daniel points to a time when the kingdom will be restored to Israel, just as we have in the Revelation. So that Daniel in the Old Testament is the corresponding book to the book of the Revelation in the New Testament.

Now in the book of Daniel there are twelve chapters. The first six are historical; the latter six are prophetical. Those first six—the historical chapters, give us the prophetic principles; the principles which God will work out in times yet to come, the latter six (from 7-12) the prophetic plan, God's scheme for bringing these principles into effect. It is, by the way, very interesting to notice that at the end of Daniel chapter 7 in the original language there is a change; the first seven chapters are mainly in Syriac (Chaldee), then from the end of chapter seven onward Daniel writes in the Hebrew language. Now, of course, we can understand why that is; in chapters 1-7 he is dealing chiefly with the Gentiles so he writes in a Gentile tongue, but from chapter 8 onwards he is speaking chiefly of Israel so he takes up the Hebrew language. Thus we see the book is divinely ordered in a very wonderful and striking way.

In chapter one we have the great principle of God's faithfulness to His people. Israel was scattered, their princes were taken captive, their land was wasted, they were exiles in

DANIEL

a far off country, but God is faithful, and Daniel, Shadrach, Meshach and Abed-nego are protected by the hand of God, and there in a distant land, in an alien country, God works for their support and God brings them out triumphantly—it is the principle of the faithfulness of God. Now, beloved, the nation had been unfaithful, the nation had rebelled against God, but God is sovereignly and wonderfully faithful. That is one of the principles we are going to see in days to come—we, as Christians see it now, but prophetically, on the earth, Israel is going to see it bye and bye. When the Church has gone there will be a remnant of Israel that is saved—144,000 in the time of tribulation, and they will prove the faithfulness of God. Chapter one then teaches us the faithfulness of God to His people. When we turn to chapter two we see God's purposes towards the world. In this chapter Nebuchadnezzar has a dream, it is a dream of an image—we shall not go into details now, but Daniel says that image represents four kingdoms—four world empires that are to arise, and then he adds when they have all arisen—then—the Lord Jesus will come as the stone without hands, and He will fill the world with His glory and the whole wide world will acknowledge His sovereignty. To repeat then—Chapter 1 God's faithfulness to His people; Chapter 2 His purposes for the world. Then, in chapter three we have God glorifying Himself. Shadrach, Meshach and Abed-nego were faithful to God and they would not bow to Nebuchadnezzar's image, and so in his anger Nebuchadnezzar took those three Hebrew heroes and cast them into the furnace, but the Lord was there in the furnace, and God delivered them from Nebuchadnezzar's power and triumphed over him, and the king was made to realise that God is the only true God—so God glorified Himself. Beloved, in days to come, when the Church is no longer here—in the tribulation—God will compel the nations to acknowledge His glory, and in the millenium God will set His glory in the earth and the whole universe will

CHAPTER 1

acknowledge that God is supreme and sovereign, and it is then that the title of God will come out in all its strength—El Elyon—the Most High God. He will be acknowledged in the millenium as the Most High God. (You will remember the first time we read of this wonderful title is in Genesis 14 when Melchizedek is brought before us as a priest of the Most High God. So when the Lord comes out in the millenium as the Melchizedek priest—priest and king—then God will be magnified as the Most High God. However, that is getting a little away from our point).

Well now, chapter 3 brings before us the principle of God glorifying Himself; chapter 4 brings out the principle of God humbling the kings of the earth. In the fourth chapter Nebuchadnezzar looks out upon his palace and his city, and swelling with pride he says "This is great Babylon that I have built", and so God smote him and he turned like a beast to eat the grass of the field until seven times passed over him, until that time came when he said "And at the end of the days, I, Nebuchadnezzar, lifted up mine eyes unto heaven, and mine understanding returned unto me and I blessed the Most High and I praised and honoured Him that liveth for ever, whose dominion is an everlasting dominion and His kingdom is from generation to generation, and all the inhabitants of the earth are reputed as nothing; and He doeth according to His will in the army of heaven, and among the inhabitants of the earth; and none can stay his hand or say unto Him what doest Thou". God humbled the great monarch of the earth—well, in a coming day God is going to humble the great monarchs again. In that day the empires that have been and gone will be revived—Babylon, Medo-Persia, Greece, Rome, Assyria, Egypt—all the empires which once had their heyday and now have waned, they will all be revived again and the whole purpose of them will be that they might be humbled before God, be brought low, and acknowledge His sovereignty. Speaking of coming times Luke (ch. 21 v 29) says "Behold the fig tree and all the

DANIEL

trees" —the fig tree represents Israel, the other trees figure the Gentiles—all the trees of the field then—all the nations of the earth—are going to be humbled before God that Christ might be magnified. Now let us look back for a moment, chapter 1 brings before us God's faithfulness to His people, chapter 2 His purpose for the world, chapter 3 the principle of God glorifying Himself, chapter 4, the principle of God humbling the kings of the earth. In chapter 5 we have Babylonish blasphemy; Belshazzar impiously, irreverently, takes the holy vessels of the Lord and seeks to blaspheme God, and God humbles that king for his blasphemy—blasphemy against God.

Then in chapter 6 we have bitterness against God's people. The servants of King Darius plotted and schemed to have Daniel cast into the den of lions—bitterness against God's people. Now in the time of tribulation there will be a system in the world which God calls Babylon the Great, the Mother of Harlots—it is corrupt Christianity, false, spurious, counterfeit Christianity, notably Roman Catholicism, and that system will blaspheme God, blaspheme His Holy Name; that is the principle of chapter 5. But, then, along with that blasphemy against God there will be bitterness against God's people. So, God's people on earth, the remnant out of Israel, and those that are saved out of the Gentiles after the Church has gone, will pass through a time of terrible tribulation, because of the bitterness of the enemies of God. Blasphemy against God—chapter 5, bitterness against God's people—chapter 6.

Now we come to the second section of the book, and here we get the prophetic plan—how God is going to bring about His plan. In chapter 7 God gives the general view of the whole prophetic scheme. We have four beasts representing the four great world empires, and when they pass away a throne is set up and One sits on the throne, He is the Ancient of days—God Himself—and the Lord Jesus approaches

CHAPTER 1 37

God and there is given to Him a kingdom and great authority. Here we get the general scheme of prophecy; kingdoms will rise, will wax and wane, but at the end of it all Christ shall reign, Christ shall have dominion, and He shall be universally acknowledged. Now the last of those four beasts in chapter 7 is the Roman empire (we shall seek to deal with that, God willing, later), and out of that beast which represents the Roman empire there comes a little horn—this little horn represents the great beast that shall appear in the time of tribulation, the man of sin, the great world ruler who springs out of the Roman empire. But then in chapter 8 there is another little horn. In this chapter two beasts appear, a ram representing Medo-Persia, and a goat representing Greece, and out of that Grecian goat there comes another little horn and he also represents a world ruler, but not of Rome as in the seventh chapter, for here the Assyrian monarch is represented by the little horn of chapter 8, he is the King of the north. So we have two great characters, two great enemies of God's people; the Roman monarch of chapter 7 and the Assyrian monarch of chapter 8. The Roman monarch, the man of sin, the Assyrian monarch the king of the North.

Then, in chapter 9 we get Israel and her natural foes. This is the chapter of the seventy weeks; Daniel's famous seventy weeks prophecy. There, in that chapter we find Israel persecuted by Assyria from the north, by Egypt from the south, by Rome from the West—Israel and her natural foes. But in chapter 10 we have Israel and her spiritual foes. Daniel has been praying, praying for three weeks, and the answer has not come, and then at last the angel comes and he tells Daniel the reason why his prayer was held up. He says "the prince of the kingdom of Persia withstood me" (Daniel 10:13)—referring to a Satanic prince, a fallen angel, who came and sought to resist the angel of God and withhold him from coming to Daniel, and so for three weeks the answer to Daniel's prayer had been delayed by Satanic activity, by

38   DANIEL

spiritual war in the heavenly places. So Daniel chapter 10 gives a glimpse of Satanic power, it shows us that the Devil has legions of angels who do his bidding. The Devil has an organised heirarchy—he has some one in charge of the work here in Wales, someone in charge of the work in England, he has myrmidons and servants in charge of all his work in various parts of the world, and we get a glimpse of this ordered vile, foul, evil heirarchy of Satan in chapter 10, warring against God and warring against His people. So, to repeat, in chapter 9 we have Israel and her natural foes; in chapter 10, Israel and her spiritual foes. Then, in chapter 11 we get the course of prophecy.

In chapter 11 we get a divine revelation of the conflict of two great nations. Palestine was a little buffer state between two great world powers, the mighty nation of Assyria to the north and the great Egyptian nation to the south; chapter 11 then tells us of the warfare of Assyria and Egypt. They made war through the centuries, and, of course, if Assyria attacked Egypt they went through Palestine, and it was so when Egypt attacked Assyria, thus Palestine was the centre of warfare for centuries, and this was where the people of God were, a little country between two mighty forces to the south and in the north and whenever those giant nations sought to attack each other they did so through Palestine and in the process ravished the land. Well now, chapter 11 takes us through the whole history of it and carries on right to the coming day, showing that in the tribulation Assyria and Egypt will unite together against the monarch of Rome, and they will pour into the land of Palestine and there will be that great battle of Armageddon, then God will come in to deliver His people. So chapter 11 gives the whole course of prophecy from the past right on to the future when the Lord will appear for the deliverance of His people. Chapter 11 then gives us the course of prophecy and is followed in chapter 12 with the conclusion of prophecy. Chapter 12 takes us to the end of it all, and the great purposes of God, of how God is going to

CHAPTER 1

39

honour and exalt His Son—showing that all prophecy is directed to God's glory. God says to Daniel—"Go thou thy way till the end be; for thou shalt rest and stand in thy lot at the end of the days" (Daniel 12:13)—just go on your way, Daniel, God will work out His purposes, and bye and bye your body will rest in the tomb—but—you will rise again and stand in your lot (i.e. in your inheritance) at the appointed time, when God has worked things out to the praise and glory of His Name. Here in these twelve chapters we have a very ordered outline:—

Chapter 1. God's faithfulness to His people.
Chapter 2. His purposes for the world.
Chapter 3. God glorifying Himself.
Chapter 4. God humbling the kings of the earth.
Chapter 5. Blasphemy against God.
Chapter 6. Bitterness against His people.
Chapter 7. The little horn out of the Roman empire.
Chapter 8. The little horn out of the Grecian empire.
Chapter 9. Israel and her natural foes.
Chapter 10. Israel and her spiritual foes.
Chapter 11. The course of prophecy.
Chapter 12. The conclusion of prophecy.

All these things beautifully outlined for us in God's wonderful blessed Word.

Having said that then, I want to turn to Daniel Chapter 1. In this chapter there are three things in particular which I would like to bring before you. In verses 1 and 2 we have a **conquered people**—Nebuchadnezzar came and conquered Jerusalem and destroyed it—a conquered people. In verses 3 to 7 we have **captured princes**—Daniel and his fellows Shadrach, Meshach and Abed-nego captured by their enemies. From verse 8 to the end of the chapter we have a **consecrated purpose**—Daniel's purpose (with the others) not to eat the King's meat. "In the third year of the reign of

40   DANIEL

Jehoiakim king of Judah"—Jehoiakim you know was the man to whom Jeremiah sent the Word of God (Jeremiah 36) and he took scissors and cut it up. Now in his reign the kingdom was taken from him—the man who rejected God's Word. When Israel rejected the Word of God they lost the kingdom, and many years afterwards, about 500 years, they rejected the Son of God, and then they lost their land, and for nearly two thousand years they were driven from their own land of Palestine. In the book of Jeremiah they rejected the Word of God and lost the kingdom; in the gospels they rejected the Son of God and they lost their land. "Came Nebuchadnezzar king of Babylon into Jerusalem and besieged it and the Lord gave Jehoiakim king of Judah into his hand with part of the vessels of the house of God"

Here is Nebuchadnezzar king of Babylon and he comes and seeks to destroy the land of Palestine. Look, fellow believers, in the Old Testament we read of Assyria, Babylon and Egypt—and they all represent the world—Assyria represents the world materially; Egypt represents the world morally; Babylon represents the world religiously. Assyria the land of might and strength and power with those ruthless men Sennacherib and Rab Shakeh—representing the world in its material might and power. Egypt where the Israelites were tempted to worship the gods of Egypt, where they sat by the flesh pots. Egypt where they drank of the water from beneath (in Palestine they drank of the water from above—in Egypt the water from beneath—the river Nile). Egypt representing the world morally. Babylon—the first time we read (in particular) of Babylon is in Genesis chapter 11, where they marched into the plain of Shinar, and they built the tower of Babel (and Babel means confusion). Beloved, in the world's religion there is all kind of confusion—there are multitudes of religions in the world, one says one thing another says another thing and there is a hopeless Babel—it is the confusion of the world's religion. In Babel we have the exaltation of men—"Go to (they said) let

CHAPTER 1   41

us build us a tower let us make us a name"—it is the exaltation of men, and in the world's religious systems that is what we always have. Let me say this gently and kindly, but, beloved, in the world's religions they always lead to the elevation of men—clergy and laity, a higher and a lower, a superior and an inferior; the world's religions have always worked in that way, towards the exaltation of man. Again, if we turn to the New Testament, and to Revelation 17 we have a picture of corrupt, counterfeit Christianity, notably Roman Catholicism—a woman sits on seven hills, the city of Rome is built on seven hills; she is drunken with the blood of martyrs, the history of Romanism teems with martyrdom; her name is called Mystery, Roman Catholicism is a mystery religion, a secret religion, she has colours, scarlet and so on, the very colours which the cardinals of Rome wear today; well there is that vivid picture of her in Revelation 17 and God calls her "Babylon the Great, the Mother of Harlots"—Babylon in scripture always stands for that which is corrupt, worthless, evil, satanic, that which is of man and not of God, in the things of God. Babylon is the picture of the world's religion in contrast with that which is of God.

Now Nebuchadnezzar king of Babylon came in here, and he impoverished Israel, he took away their treasure, he took away their vessels, he took away their temple. The world's religious systems will always impoverish us, will make us spiritually poor, will take from us that which we have got. Oh, child of God, I do ask of you—in everything of your spiritual life rest upon the Word of God, build your faith upon what God has written in His Word. Remember, if we turn aside from God, if we turn from the order of scripture and embrace the order of man—we shall always be spiritually impoverished. You know there is a tendency even among God's people today, when spiritual questions crop up to say, "I, think this, or I, think that" or "what do you make of this and that"—reasoning out, trying to evolve by logical processes all manner of things, instead of simply building

42   DANIEL

upon the Word of God, instead of taking God's Word as it is. You know, I often long for the days when I was a boy, when I went with my father to the meeting and I used to see the elder brethren when things cropped up in the meeting or things were suggested—their invariable reply was "Brother, is it in the Book—have you got a thus-said-the-Lord for it?" I also remember a man who came in to my father's shop in an effort to teach my father some very strange doctrine—and he would often remark to my father "Here's the whole thing in a nutshell" but my father would retort "Aye, you have given it to me in a nutshell, but now, can you give it to me in the Book?"

So we see here how this vile Babylonish system came in and impoverished the people of God, and if we depart from Divine order we too shall be impoverished. Let us take a point from the Roman Catholic system to which we have already referred—you and I are encouraged to read the Bible and to get light from it, but the Roman religion says "No, you can only approach the Bible through the teachings of the fathers", and they put the teaching of the fathers between the people and the Word of God. You and I believe we can feed on Christ—Rome says "No, the only way to do that is to receive a wafer consecrated by the priest"— and they put the ornate garments of their priesthood, their wafers and such like, between us and our Blessed Lord. Again, you and I believe that when we are saved we can confess to the Lord and be forgiven; Roman Catholicism substitutes confession to the priest. So you see, fellow believers, the whole object of Rome is to put buttresses between us and God until all we can see of God is what we can discern from the stained glass windows of the churches. Man's systems will always rob us and leave us poor. There was a man on the Jericho road, and the priest and the Levite passed by on the other side—man's systems impoverish and wither the soul of God's people. So we find with Babylon.

Now let us look at the next section—verses 3 to 7—where

CHAPTER 1

we read about captured princes. ("And they got some of the King's seed" —captured princes). Nebuchadnezzar, king of Babylon looked round for the best men in Israel; he instructed his servant Ashpenaz to seek the men that were clever, able, skilful,—"I want them," said the king—and so he took the best men out of Israel—Daniel, Shadrach, Meshach and Abednego and he takes them for himself—to be his servants. Beloved, the Devil is always seeking to get the best of your skill and mine—he seeks to come in and lure away princes with ability, and to get them for himself. He does not want our talent to go for the Lord, he wishes it for himself. We read as, in I Samuel 14, v.52 that when Saul, Satan's man, became king of Israel, he looked for all that were clever, all that were valiant, all that were mighty—and he got them for himself. But what a contrast when David came to reign (see I Samuel 22 v.2), "there went out to David, the poor, the distressed that were in debt." Saul collected the able and the mighty men; David the poor and wretched—and the Bible says "God has chosen the weak things, the base things, the things that are not"—the Devil goes in for the able, the clever; God takes the weak, the poor, and the base. Ah, but you know the point is this—God takes the poor, the base, and the things that are not—but they do not remain like that—the marvellous thing is that when men and women come to Christ, they might be ignorant, unable to read or write, having no ability in the things of this world, but how many times we have seen instances of God taking such men in hand, and the Lord has made gentlemen of them, given them ability, education, learning, things they never had before—then when the Devil sees these men coming to Christ and being changed—learning politeness, manners, being educated, he covets them for himself. God has saved them, God has reared them, advanced them, built them up, then the Devil tries to attract those people to himself.

Maybe I put that very vaguely, but to illustrate; in the

44 DANIEL

meeting at _____ there was a lad of the roughest type I had ever seen, a veritable ignoramus, as rough as could be, devoid of education, unable to read or write, but schooled in such things as gambling and the like. The Lord saved him, Christ came into his life, and God took up this object, poor, mean, base and wretched, and in the school of Christ he became a different man. He learned to read and write, learned to be respectable, upright; he was a transformed man. Ah, but then the Devil looked upon him and regarded his new abilities; he attracted him to trade unionism, and today he is a trade union official, far away from God. One day I met him and kindly reminded him of God's refining process in him; he fully acknowledged this, and I was moved to tell him plainly how he was using for the Devil all that God had given him. Now that was the case with these princes in Israel, God had made them all that they were, and the Devil sought them for himself, sought to make them servants of the king of Babylon. Young men and women, intellectual, clever, refined, respectable, upright—all that you have you got from God, you owe it to the Lord Jesus Christ—may I urge you earnestly never to give it to the Devil. The Devil wants you, he wants your ability, your knowledge, your cleverness, he wants these for himself, but, dear child of God, do not let him have them, keep those things which God has given you, and give them back to God.

Well now, secondly, the Devil sought by Nebuchadnezzar to destroy Christ-likeness in these men who were called Daniel, Mishael, Hananiah and Azariah, all names which speak of God ("El" and "Iah" are abbreviations of the word meaning God). Their four names spoke of God but Nebuchadnezzar sought to change that, to blot out from their lives the reference to God—Daniel he named Belteshazzar after Bel the Babylonian god, and the others he called Shadrach, Meshach, Abed-nego, giving them the names of heathen gods, so to blot out from them the things of Jehovah and make them conform to these strange gods.

CHAPTER 1

So beloved, we see the Devil's object to blot out the things of Christ from our lives, to destroy in the Christian life every vestige of Christ-likeness and to be conformed to this world, but what does the Word say? "Be not conformed to this world, but be transformed by the renewing of your minds, that ye may prove what is that good and acceptable and perfect will of God".

Now let us look at the last section where we read about a consecrated purpose (verse 8). "But Daniel purposed in his heart that he would not defile himself with a portion of the king's meat". It was the custom in Babylon for the king to offer his meat first to idols, now the four young men were offered the king's meat—what a privilege to be served with the king's meat—ah, but the king's meat had been offered to idols, so Daniel says "No" to it, they could not touch that, and he refused to partake of it. God keep us, too, from feeding on the food of the world, the idolatrous food. I Corinthians 10:20 says, "The things that the Gentiles sacrifice they sacrifice to demons and not to God"—God keep you and me from feeding on the things of the world. I say this lovingly, but, oh it burns in my heart to see, as I go about, dear young Christians feeding on these trashy, shallow novels or spending hours glued to the television and looking at all that rubbish which comes over on it, and generally feeding on the things of the world. Beloved, God has called you out, and given Christ to be our soul-food, God grant we shall not defile ourselves with the king's meat. I was telling the folk last week of a man whose family had persuaded him to get a television into the house, but when the thing arrived in its big box he observed that it had upon it the telling inscription "Brings the world into your house". "The world into my house," he mused, and so out it went as soon as it had arrived. Let us seek to keep the world out of our homes and lives.

So they would not defile themselves with the king's meat, these young Hebrews ate the pure food. They fed on pulse and water, and feeding on the right food had a threefold result; (1) It made them beautiful (after ten days Melzar found they were more beautiful than the Babylonians). (2) It made them wise (we read that Daniel had skill and understanding). (3) It led to advancement (Nebuchadnezzar advanced them in the kingdom). In like manner, feeding on the food of God will make us beautiful—dear young sisters, let me say to you, you cannot buy beauty at the chemist shop or the hairdressers, but you can be spiritually, radiantly beautiful if you feed upon the things of God. It brings out what God calls the beauty of holiness. Feeding upon God's Word will also make you wise in the things of God, and feeding upon the things of God will lead to advancement in the Kingdom. So feeding upon divine things may mean that you will some day hear the call of God, and you may be sent to India, Africa or somewhere else in His service. Feeding on the right things then leads to beauty, wisdom and advancement.

Daniel Chapter 2

Mr. Bell read Daniel chapter 2

I want you to think of chapter 2 in two sections; (1) In verses 1-23 we have the revelation **to** Daniel. Nebuchadnezzar had a dream and the dream had gone from him and he wanted somebody to reveal what he had dreamed; and the interpretation of it. In answer to prayer God gave a revelation to Daniel. (2) Then from verse 24 to the end of the chapter Daniel comes to Nebuchadnezzar and unfolds to him this revelation, so it is the revelation **through** Daniel.

In verses 1-23 mention is made of the God of Heaven, it says that Daniel and his friends Hananiah, Mishael and Azariah desired mercies of the God of Heaven. Now in the second half of the chapter Daniel speaks about the God **in** Heaven Who can reveal these things. Perhaps I should pause at this point and say something about that expression, occuring several times in this chapter—"the God of Heaven". We never read this expression in the Bible until the Jews were taken into captivity, but after Nebuchadnezzar came and took Judah into captivity, then we read of the "God of Heaven" — for instance Cyrus said in Ezra chapter 1 "the God of Heaven hath given me a kingdom". Now why is that? It is because God had no place on earth. God had taken up Israel as His nation but they had turned aside from God unto idols. They had rejected God and now God had no more place on earth. However, although He is shut out from affairs on earth, yet He is working His purposes; He is accomplishing His will and shall accomplish it until all is brought to a satisfactory

47

48   DANIEL

conclusion. Cowper, the famous poet said, "God's in His heaven all's right with the world," but you know Cowper had rather the wrong idea, it is because God is in His heaven that all's wrong with the world.

Let us consider the first part of the chapter verses 1-23. There are just one or two expressions there that I want to bring before you. Verse 2 "Then the king commanded to call the magicians and the astrologers and the sorcerers and the Chaldeans". Now Nebuchadnezzar had had a dream; a dream with a message, but he had forgotten it, he could not remember it, and he wanted somebody to recall the dream and to reveal it. So he called these men, the magicians were men of supernatural power, men who, by the devil, had supernatural ability. The astrologers were star-gazers and professed to get messages from the stars. The sorcerers were tricksters using devilish trickery and deception. The Chaldeans were wise men, from the land of Chaldea, noted for wisdom. Nebuchadnezzar arranges these men before him and asks them to reveal the dream that he had had in the past and to reveal its message for the future, and they can do neither; they are absolutely at a loss. We need never be afraid of the truth of the Bible; we hear of wise and eminent men, denying it but remember, the wisdom of this world has its limits and can only go so far. "In the Cross of Christ" we read in I Corinthians chapter 2 "God hath made void the wisdom of this world". The wisdom of this world has been condemned in the Cross of Christ. So if supposed scientists and philosophers and learned men deny the Word of God, if they belittle its teaching, we need not worry too much for their knowledge and wisdom is at the best limited, but God's is an infinite wisdom. God's is a knowledge that shall never pass away. (I think the wisdom of man was well defined in the description of a philosopher as being like a blind man in a dark room looking for a black cat that is not there.) So we need not bother about the world's wisdom but rest confidently on the Word of God.

CHAPTER 2

49

"I need no other argument,
I need no other plea,
It is enough that Jesus died,
And that He died for me."

Now look down the chapter to verse 10, "The Chaldeans answered before the king, and said, there is not a man upon the earth than can show the king's matter; therefore there is no king, lord or ruler, that asked such things at any magician, or astrologer, or Chaldean. And it is a rare thing that the king requireth, and there is none other that can show it before the king, except the gods, whose dwelling is not with flesh." Notice particularly the answer of these magicians of the king, "there is no man on earth that can reveal this". Their thoughts were of the earth. Now the Scripture says concerning Satan's wisdom that it is earthly, sensual, devilish, belonging to earth and not to heaven. When Saul of Tarsus was converted, in Acts chapter 9 it says, "There shone upon him a light from heaven," but the devil's wisdom, God says, is earthly, sensual and devilish. The contrast is between the earthly and the heavenly. Of course the Chaldeans were right, they did not look beyond the earth. Then they said, "the only one who knows these things are the gods and the dwelling of the gods is not with men". Notice what heathendom believes: the only one who can answer your questions are the gods. The god of the heathen is removed and far away; the heathen says my god is aloof, removed, distant, he is out of my ken altogether, he is far away. They have no access, no fellowship, with their idols, but, of you and I, fellow believers, the Bible says, "You who were sometimes far off are made nigh by the blood of Christ". Our God is not removed, He is not aloof, He is not distant, He is very near to us and we can say, "He walks with me and He talks with me and He tells me I am His own, and the joy we share as we tarry there, none other has ever known." We have been brought into intimate and immediate

50

DANIEL

contact with the living God.

Then we read of fellowship in prayer. Nebuchadnezzar gave an order that all the magicians should be destroyed because they could not tell his dream. Why so? These men had served Nebuchadnezzar for years as magicians, but now he is beginning to see through them and he says he knows their treachery. If they knew his dream they would concoct a lie as to its interpretation, but how does he come to see through them? Oh beloved, chapter 2 follows chapter 1. Earlier in chapter 1 we saw Daniel and his friends, the three young men, and we saw their godly, saintly life, we saw their devout character. They went in before Nebuchadnezzar, and Nebuchadnezzar sees something that he had never seen before, he sees the people of God; he sees God's glory manifest in these holy men of God. It would seem, that from that time onwards Nebuchadnezzar began to have doubts about his astrologers and magicians and Chaldeans and so forth. He had seen the light of heaven in the faces of Daniel, Shadrach, Meshach and Abed-nego and it had turned his thought towards heaven. Oh beloved, God grant that you and I may so live, so manifest Christ, so tell out His glory that many a sceptic, many an unbeliever, may be delivered from their falsehood and error. Peter says, "that with well doing ye might put to silence the ignorance of foolish men". Up in Chirnside in Scotland in the last century there lived David Hulme the great agnostic; he was a man of a wonderful mind, a man of tremendous ability, but one that did not believe in anything. He even doubted his own existence and was inclined to think that perhaps the world was unreal and he was unreal and there was nothing real. His mother had been one who acknowledged God and David Hulme tried to talk his mother out of any belief in God. One day she wrote to him and said, "David, you took away all that I had but you gave me nothing back". Some time later, sitting in his drawing room, and looking through the window with a friend, he saw a young man cross the green.

CHAPTER 2 51

The young man was well known in the village of Chirnside as a saintly and noble lad, and he was going to the Scottish Kirk with his Bible under his arm. David Hulme, turning to his friend said, "That is the only argument for Christianity for which I have no answer; I can answer any argument for Christianity except that; I cannot answer the saintliness of that young man." Oh beloved, the saintliness of those who walk with the Lord, who live in the fellowship of the Lord Jesus Christ, is an answer, a repudiation of all the infidelity of men, that nobody can answer. It puts to silence, as Peter says, "the ignorance of foolish men".

Now, as I remarked we find something here about prayer. First we read about patience in prayer. Here is Daniel entering into a partnership with his three friends, verse 14. Daniel answered with counsel and wisdom to Arioch the captain of the king's guard, and asked "Why is the king's decree so hasty? Then Daniel went in and desired of the king that he would give him time, and he would show the king the interpretation. Here we see Daniel in patient prayer. In the face of a great calamity, Daniel seeks time to spread the matter before God in prayer, confident that God will give him the answer. Beloved, God give us patience in prayer. "Though years have passed since first praying, do not despair, The Lord will answer you sometime, somewhere". Sometimes we come to God and present our prayers before Him, and, if we do not get an immediate answer, we drop the matter. Not so with Daniel; he continues to pray, knowing that the answer would come. Thus we see his **patience in prayer.** Verse 17 Then Daniel went into his house and made the thing known unto Hananiah, Mishael, and Azariah, his companions, that they would desire mercies of the God of Heaven concerning the secret, that Daniel and his fellows should not perish with the rest of the wise men of Babylon. Then was the secret revealed to Daniel in a night vision. Then Daniel blessed the God of Heaven". Oh, beloved, here is **power in prayer.** Those four men joined together,

52   DANIEL

persisting with God, and their prayers prevailed, and the hand of God was moved. Lastly, there was **praise in prayer,** v.20, "Daniel answered and said, Blessed be the name of God for ever and ever." Thus we have seen patience in prayer, power in prayer, and praise in prayer. (How important it is when our prayers are answered, that we, like Daniel, should thank, praise and honour God).

Now we come to verse 24 and the second part of the chapter. "Therefore Daniel went in unto Arioch whom the king had ordained to destroy the wise men of Babylon: he went and said thus unto him; Destroy not the wise men of Babylon: bring me in before the king, and I will show unto the king the interpretation". Verse 27, "Daniel answered in the presence of the king" and he told the king first of all three things. First, the **source of revelation,** "The secret which the king had demanded, cannot the wise men, the astrologers, the magicians, the soothsayers shew unto the king". He told him the source of the revelation. Nebuchadnezzar, the answer to your problem is not with the wise men, the astrologers, the soothsayers, it is not from them that revelation comes; the source of revelation is God. Oh beloved, that you and I may know this, that the answer to all our spiritual and moral problems, the answer to all that is vital and essential in the lives of God's people, is found in God Himself. So often there is a tendency to build up our lives, to build up our habits and our conduct on our own thoughts, and our own ideas, on the world's philosophies, on the ethics of men. Daniel says, there is a **source** of revelation, it is God Himself. God grant that His word, His scripture, His holy ordained revelation may be the path by which we shall always walk. "Trust in the Lord with all thine heart, and lean not unto thine own understanding. In all thy ways acknowledge Him and He shall direct thy paths."

Then in verses 28 and 29 we get the **substance of revelation.** "But there is a God in Heaven that revealeth secrets, and maketh known to the king Nebuchadnezzar

CHAPTER 2 53

what shall be in the latter days" and in verse 29 "... maketh known to thee what shall come to pass". Thus in verse 27 we have the Source of Revelation, in verses 28 and 29 the Substance of Revelation. Oh, beloved, God, the great God of inscrutable, matchless wisdom, He is taking you and me into His confidence, how wonderful. Though we are as but grasshoppers in His sight, though the nations are but as a drop in the bucket, though He taketh up the isles as a very little thing, yet He is taking you and me into His confidence. He has revealed His mind to us and He has revealed to us in His Word, the things that are going to come to pass. Fellow believers, how kind of God, how wonderfully kind, to enlighten poor human creatures like you and me, to take us into His counsel and enlighten us concerning all His divine purposes. You know, the sad thing is that, although God has done this, so many of us neglect this revelation: we neglect this prophetic unfolding and yet God has been so wonderfully gracious to take us into His counsel concerning things that are coming to pass.

Well, we have had the source of revelation and the substance of revelation but now in verse 30 we get the **Secret of Revelation**. "But as for me, this secret is not revealed to me for any wisdom that I have more than any living, but for their sakes that shall make known the interpretation to the king, and that thou mightest know the thougths of thy heart." The whole substance of revelation is to reveal ourselves **to us**, to show us how unworthy we are, "That thou mayest know the thoughts of **thine** heart": the whole object of revelation is to bring us down on our faces before God, that we might have no confidence in ourselves and that the Lamb may be all the glory. We take the book of the Revelation, the last book of the Bible; twenty-eight times it mentions the Lamb: the whole object of that book is to display the glories of Christ in order, that as God's glory is revealed, you and I might know the secrets of our hearts, and finding out our unworthiness, finding our wretchedness, we

54   DANIEL

might fall on our faces and ascribe all the glory to the Lord Jesus Christ. Many years ago, when I was quite young, I was travelling to a meeting by bus, and an old, florid faced gentleman, who was next to me across the aisle, engaged me in conversation. Very soon we were talking of what he termed "religion". He condemned the churches and chapels as all being wrong. "Well", I said, "You know what the need is, Sir, it is to get back to the cross of Christ (who died for the ungodly); the message of the Bible." That brought out the old gentlemen in absolute fury — "Away with that", he said, "You ought to read my book — the Plain Man's Philosophy of Life." Then he went on "Look at John and the Revelation, why the book of Revelation is only a fantasy." We talked for a little while until the bus approached Durham, where I had to change, and I just turned to the old man and said, as my parting comment, "Listen, Sir; you speak of the Revelation being a fantasy, but do you know why that book is so precious to me? It closes with these words — Surely I come quickly — closing with an assurance that my Lord is coming for me. That is why I love the book, because every day I have this glorious hope that perhaps this very day Christ may come for me." The old gentleman broke down, and sobbed in the bus, as he put out his great big hands to grasp mine, and as he held me warmly, he said, "My boy, I'd love to have such a hope; I'd love to have such a Saviour". Oh, beloved, it is the revelation of God; God manifest in Christ, revealing the hearts of men to themselves, and bringing them down before God. Said Paul in I Corinthians 14 "If one that is unlearned or an unbeliever come in, the secrets of his heart will be manifest, and falling on his face, he will claim that God is among you of a truth." God manifest — man upon his face.

Well now, from verse 27 to verse 30 we have **Daniel's introduction**, and then from verse 31 we have **Daniel's instruction** in two parts. In verses 31 to 35 we have the revelation of the **secrets of the king;** he tells Nebuchadnezzar

CHAPTER 2

what he dreamed. Then from verse 36 to the end of the chapter we have the revelation of the **secrets of God;** here Daniel tells Nebuchadnezzar what God is going to do. Look at verse 37 Nebuchadnezzar has had a dream and has seen an image, with a head of gold, breast and arms of silver, a body of brass, legs of iron, feet of iron and clay. From verse 37 Daniel interprets this dream. "Thou O King, art a king of kings, for the God of Heaven hath given thee a kingdom, power and strength and glory," and at the end of verse 38, "Thou art this head of gold". Now Nebuchadnezzar is told that his image represents four nations, four great world empires: yet it is only one image; why is that? Because there is just one divine purpose going through all history. Nations rise and fall but there is one divine purpose running through them all.

So these four empires are represented by one image because it is one single purpose of God that links them altogether. This image represented four world empires and they gradually deteriorate, first it is gold, then it is silver, then brass, then iron, then iron and clay; it is getting lower and lower and lower. Gold is more valuable than silver, silver more valuable than brass, brass more valuable than iron, iron more valuable than clay. It is deteriorating, beloved, the world is not getting any better: our Lord said, "things shall wax worse and worse". "But thou O King, art that head of gold". Nebuchadnezzar was an absolute ruler. Now none of the empires after him has ever had the same complete authority. The Medes and Persian kings could not do anything contrary to the law of their counsellors. If a law of the Medes and Persians was established even the king was bound by it. Nebuchadnezzar was not like that; he was his own law-giver, and he could make and alter laws as he wished. He had absolute control. Alexander the Great was governed in a measure by his four generals. The Caesars of Rome were governed by the consulate but Nebuchadnezzar was an absolute complete ruler — "Thou art that head of

DANIEL

gold," and so Daniel tells Nebuchadnezzar that all his glory, all his temples of Babylon, all his wonderful learning, all his marvellous hanging gardens, all his mighty river Euphrates, the river of sweet water, all his far flung dominions, all his expensive kingdom, all his worldwide imperialistic power — all — came from God; and God is the source of all that he has.

Then Daniel says, "after thee shall come three other kingdoms, inferior to thee". First the kingdom of silver, then the kingdom of brass, then the kingdom of iron. Now who are these kingdoms? Well, beloved, God has not left us in any doubt about this. It is not what we think it is, not what history says, it is what God says in His word. The shoulder and breasts and arms of silver represent the Medo-Persian empire. There were two countries, Media and Persia and they formed a joint united government, Media and Persia together, and they called it the Medo-Persian empire. Now that was the empire that followed Nebuchadnezzar. How do we know that? Because when we turn to Daniel chapter 8 (where we read of the empires to succeed Babylon) Daniel sees a ram and God says to him "The ram which thou sawest having two horns are the kings of Media and Persia", so we have divine authority for saying that this second empire, the shoulder and breasts of silver, was the Medo-Persian empire. Then there was the body of brass: again we have divine authority for saying that this was the Grecian empire, because in chapter 8 we read of a goat and God says "The rough goat is the king of Grecia".

Here is God unfolding the world's history. Daniel tells Nebuchadnezzar, the world monarch, that when he passed away there will be a series of world monarchs. First, the monarchs of the combined kingdom of Media and Persia and when that passes away there will be another monarch, the king of Greece, and these (Babylon, Medo-Persia and Greece) will be three world empires." Then we come down to the legs of the image which were made of iron. Well here is

CHAPTER 2   57

the fourth world power. Who is that? Again, fellow believers, we need not have doubt about this for God tells us in His word. As you know the Greek Empire was followed by the Roman and in the gospel of Luke chapter 2 we read "There went forth a decree from Caesar Augustus that **all the world** should be taxed." If we read the next chapter it says "our Lord came forth in the fifteenth year of Tiberias Caesar". So then the fourth world empire, the empire of iron, was the empire of Rome. Now there is a special force of meaning and significance to this expression 'Iron'. Daniel says that iron breaks in pieces and tears asunder and it speaks of a mighty empire. Well, the Roman empire was of tremendous strength, they had far greater military might than any empire that had come before them and it is remarkable how iron was the outstanding metal of the Roman empire. Their armaments and weapons were made of iron; that was why they were able to conquer so many other nations whose armaments and weapons were vastly inferior. Well, here we have the Roman empire, the empire of iron; this empire is also likened unto the two legs of the image. The Roman empire in its history had two divisions, the Roman empire of the east having its centre in Alexandria and the Roman empire in the west having its centre in Rome. If you go back to your school days you will remember that Mark Anthony for a time was emperor in the east while Octavian was the emperor in the west. After the western empire perished the eastern empire still carried on for a time with its centre in Constantinople. So here we get the two legs of iron representing the twofold Roman Empire as it was in historic times. Now there comes a great change.

Up until this point we have been thinking of the past but now we come to the future. Daniel takes us to the future and he shows us the **feet** of the image. The feet are of iron and clay, and when we get down to the feet we turn from history to prophecy, because it says, "There came **a stone without hands** and it struck the image on the feet." Now the stone

58 DANIEL

without hands represents our Lord coming in Glory; coming in government, coming to rule the world as He will do one day. Yes, and He strikes the image on the feet. So the legs of the image represent Rome of the past, the feet of the image represent Rome of the future. Now notice, there is no interval between the legs and feet, they are united; no interval is mentioned. God goes straight on from the Rome of the past to the Rome of the future. Beloved, when we turn to Revelation 13 God says, "The Beast that thou sawest **was, and is not;**" there is no Roman empire today; "**yet shall be,**" it is going to be revived. The legs of the image then represent Rome of the past, the feet of the image represent Rome of the future, when the Roman empire will be revived. You notice that God passes over this age. You and I live in an interval between the Rome of the past the the Rome of the future. Our Lord died on the cross and brought in the age of grace and He is gathering up out of the woıld a heavenly people, but God says nothing about that here; He steps right from the past to the future. He steps right from the Rome of the historic past to the Rome of the prophetic future. God passes this age over altogether; now why is that? It is because here God is dealing with **the earth,** He is telling Nebuchadnezzar about earthly kingdoms. Today God is not dealing with **the earth,** God is taking out of the world **a heavenly people,** so in Daniel's prophecy He passes over this age entirely. He has nothing to say about it, it is an interval in the purposes of God. As the late Mr. Fereday used to say, "the prophetic clock stopped when Christ died on the Cross, and it will start again when the Church goes home to be with the Lord". You and I are living in an interval between the legs and feet of Daniel's image and once God has removed His heavenly Church He will start to work again on earth and then will come in the feet of the revived Roman empire as it shall be by and by. Mr. J.N. Darby used to say that "the slow train of Israel has been moved into the siding so that the Church express might go through". God steps right over this age

CHAPTER 2 59

when He is taking out of the world a heavenly people unto His glorious name.

Now, God comes down to the feet of the image and the feet are made of iron and clay. God says, "it is partly strong and partly brittle." Beloved, we read in Revelation 13 that in that day, when the Roman empire is revived, they will be under the head of the great Beast, the man of sin. It is a strong empire ruled by this great super-human man, the man of sin. Oh yes, but it is a weak empire, because it is ten kingdoms in one, and each of the kingdoms has its own will. Hence whilst there is strength in it there is weakness too. The strength of iron and the weakness of clay. Furthermore we have here a tendency that we see now in germ; we see this in bud, even in our own day. I am not very old, but I can remember in my boyhood, how we used to talk about rich people and poor people, high people and low people and various distinctive terms of society, but today that is inclined to be done away with. Men are trying to do away with the classes, to abolish all distinctions, and make rich and poor, great and small all alike. It is the age of democracy, but listen, friends, God has said that you cannot mix iron and clay and, do what they will, men in trying to make a democratic state without classes must fail: as long as this world lasts in its present state there will always be a distinction between the rich and the poor. I remember, in 1917 when the Russian revolt came in, and they were going to abolish the classes, and yet there are classes today just the same as ever; you cannot mix iron and clay. Well this democratic tendency of today is just a sign, a germ, of what is going to come in its full fruit after the Church has gone.

Here in the feet of the image then is the Roman empire of the future, partly of iron and partly of clay and God refers to its toes. Now presumably the image would have ten toes, and that symbolizes the ten kingdoms of the Roman empire that are mentioned in Revelation chapter 13. The Roman empire of the future will be an amalgamation of ten kingdoms under the authority of the 'man of sin'. Ah, but, Daniel says, "I saw a stone", Who is that stone? It is our Lord Jesus Christ, He is called in I Peter chapter 2 "the living stone" He is called in Ephesians chapter 2 "the chief corner stone". Here in Daniel He is presented as "the stone cut out without hands;" none other than the Lord Jesus. Why a stone cut out without hands? Because He is the uncreated One, He was never made. Eternal, without beginning, the stone cut out without hands, begotten as man but never created. This stone comes out of the mountain, it tells of the Lord from glory, coming from the exaltation of heaven, a stone out of the mountain coming in glory. This stone comes and smites the image upon the feet and the image is ground to dust. When the Lord comes to reign (after He has taken His church home) He is going to judge the nations of this world. There they will be persecuting His people Israel, and God will come in and judge them. In that day these four nations will all be revived: Babylon, Medo-Persia, Greece and Rome, and there they will be in all their hideousness and the "stone without hands" comes and crushes them all to powder.

Now Daniel looked on this image, he describes it as glorious and terrible, ah! that is how men looked at it, but God will judge it in its real worth. The Lord Jesus Christ when He comes (Isaiah says) will not reprove after the sight of His eyes, He will judge the hearts of men, and He will condemn the nations in that day. He will put down all authority and power and He shall reign in His splendour.

Then we read that this stone expanded until it filled the whole earth, and so when Christ has come to reign, His glory will indeed expand until it fills the whole earth, and as Isaiah says "The earth shall be filled with the knowledge of the Lord as the waters cover the sea." Then the whole wide world shall tell out His glory, and strength and honour and glory and blessing will be given to Him the reigning Lord.

When Nebuchadnezzar heard this revelation his whole attitude to Daniel changed; he promoted him and also

CHAPTER 2

promoted Shadrach, Meshach and Abed-nego. The very one who had despised them before, now honours their God and blesses them. Beloved, in that day when Christ comes to reign there will be that little Jewish remnant of whom Daniel, Shadrach, Meshach and Abed-nego are a figure, and the world that hated them will honour the God of Israel. Nebuchadnezzar who hated Daniel now honours his God, and the world that hated Israel in the tribulation shall, when Christ comes and appears on their behalf — the stone without hands — instead of hating Israel will honour them and give presents to them, and as Zechariah says in the 14th chapter of his prophecy "the kings of the earth will go to Jerusalem to keep the feast of tabernacles," and again in Zechariah 8 "Men of the Gentiles will lay hold of the skirt of him that is a Jew and they will say, let us go with thee for we have heard that God is among you of a truth." So as we see that mighty potentate changing his attitude towards the Hebrew sons, we look to that day when the attitude of the world will change towards the nation of Israel. Lord Byron said:—

"Tried to the wandering foot and weary breast
How shall you fly away and be at rest.
The wild dove has her nest, the fox its cave,
Mankind their country, Israel but the grave."

But Israel's day of tribulation and sorrow is very soon coming to an end and the world shall see the favour of the people whom they so long despised and Christ shall reign in all. Oh beloved, in the light of these things shall we not say, Amen, even so come Lord Jesus.

Daniel Chapters 3 and 4.

Mr. Bell read Daniel chapter 3 verses 1-6 and verses 16-26. Chapter 4 verses 1-3, verses 10-14, verses 28-32, and verses 34-37.

In chapter 3 we have Nebuchadnezzar and the **great image**, then in chapter 4 we have Nebuchadnezzar and the **great tree**. The great image, that is what Nebuchadnezzar thought of himself; the great tree—what God thought of Nebuchadnezzar. In chapter 3 we read that God is **able to deliver**. Shadrach, Meshach and Abed-nego said to Nebuchadnezzar "Our God is able to deliver us." In chapter 4 He is able to **de-throne**. In the last verse of chapter 4 Nebuchadnezzar says that those who are proud, those who have lifted themselves up, God is able to abase, and He had done so with the mighty king Nebuchadnezzar. Now you remember we have mentioned that these historical records of the Book of Daniel show prophetic principles, and they show principles that will come to light in the time of the great tribulation, when the Church has gone. Well we see this very markedly in chapter 3. Nebuchadnezzar the great king had set up an image of himself. Now we read in Revelation chapter 13 that in the time of tribulation, the Beast, the head of the revived Roman Empire will set up an image and his false prophet will compel all men to worship him. So here we have Nebuchadnezzar in chapter 3 setting up a golden image and compelling men to worship it; a picture of what will happen when the Church has gone, when the beast, the man of sin, will set up that great image, and his false prophet will compel all men to worship it. We read of this great image of Nebuchadnezzar that it was three score cubits high, that is sixty cubits, and that it was six cubits broad. You will notice

64

DANIEL

the number six stands out. Then again when they had to worship the image there were six kinds of musical instruments "That at what time ye hear the sound of the cornet, flute, harp, sackbut, psalter, dulcimer"—6; 6; 6. Well, you remember in Revelation chapter 13 we are told that that great beast that shall arise, that head of the revived Roman empire has the number 666. As we pointed out earlier, he is a super-man, a man outstanding above all men, a man energized by Satan, but he is not perfect, he is only 666 i.e. he is one short of perfection. Seven speaks of perfection, in the book of the Revelation everything about the Lord goes by sevens; we start with seven lamp-stands and seven stars, we go on to seven churches, we read about seven spirits, we go further and read about seven seals, seven trumpets and seven vials. In chapter 10 we have seven thunders, in chapter 12 we have a beast with seven heads, in chapter 17 we have a woman sitting on seven hills: ah yes, seven goes right through the Revelation; but this Beast, the man of sin, he is six, six, six; he is short of perfection. A wonderful man, a demonic man but not perfect, only 666.

Nebuchadnezzar compelled men to worship this image. It is the object of Satan, in the time of tribulation, to turn the worship of men from God to himself. You remember he said to the Lord, "all this I will give Thee if thou wilt fall down and worship me", that is the devil's object. Well, in that day there will be the trinity of evil, the dragon, the beast, and the false prophet, impersonating the trinity of the Godhead—Father, Son and Holy Spirit. The devil's whole aim will be to steal and to purloin the worship of God and direct it towards himself. We find Nebuchadnezzar for a time very friendly towards Shadrach, Meshach and Abednego, but when there came the moment of refusal to worship his image, his friendship was turned to hatred. Now he persecutes those whom formally he befriended. In a coming day that great Beast, the head of the revived Roman empire, will be like that; for 3½ years he will be friendly to the Jews

CHAPTERS 3 & 4   65

but at the end of that time he will break his covenant with them and persecute them: so we find these three Hebrew young men are caused to go through the fire yet God brings them through the fire and they come out safely. Look at Zechariah 13, God says of Israel in the time of Tribulation, "I will bring the third part of them through the fire and refine them as silver is refined and try them as gold is tried". Thus Shadrach, Meshach and Abed-nego are representative of that godly remnant of Israel in the time of Tribulation, that third part of Israel who will be brought through the fire and who will come out at the end of the Tribulation and will be the nucleus, the root, of the kingdom of Israel which will be established in Palestine (Now Israel). We see a picture of them in Revelation chapter 7 where we read of that one hundred and forty and four thousand, twelve thousand out of every tribe, brought through the Tribulation, brought through the fire, to God's praise and glory.

Here we have a picture of things as they shall be in the Tribulation: Nebuchadnezzar the king, setting up an image and getting people to worship it, the significant number six; we see him first befriending the children of Israel and then turning against them. Then in Shadrach, Meshach and Abed-nego we have the figure of that remnant brought through the Tribulation; then at the end of chapter 3 we have Nebuchadnezzar acknowledging and proclaiming the glory of the God of Shadrach, Meshach, and Abed-nego. So also at the end of the Tribulation Christ will appear, Christ will be manifest, and God's glory will fill the whole earth. What a wonderful, a marvellous picture. By the way, fellow believers, we can see the subtlety of sin here, Nebuchadnezzar sets up an image of gold; we saw in chapter 2 that Daniel said to him, "Thou, O King art that head of gold" — the greatest of the four world empires. So Nebuchadnezzar says in effect, if I am the head of gold I will have a golden image to display my glory and exalt myself. You see how he takes even divine truth, divine revelation,

5

66   DANIEL

and he uses it to his own vanity; he uses it to his own self exaltation. When God tells him that he is the head of gold, he decides to build a great golden image to himself and get all the people to worship him. Oh, beloved, is not sin subtle; is not pride a subtle thing? Yet you know, it is possible in the Christian life, for you and me to be proud like that. It is possible for us to be proud of our prayers, proud of our spirituality, proud of our service, proud of our gift, yes, and pride can creep in, in the most unexpected ways. So Nebuchadnezzar takes even the divine revelation and uses it to his own self glorification.

Now, having tried to look at the prophetic side of Daniel chapter 3 I want to turn to the moral side of it. These things have a practical moral lesson, something which comes down to the present day; moral and spiritual pictures which affect our own lives. Shadrach, Meshach and Abed-nego are brought before the king, and the king commands that they worship this image, but they say "We will not worship thine image, O king". Now, there is a divine principle here. God tells you and me in Romans 13 to be subject to the powers that be, and that we must be subject to every ordinance of man. Ah, but, God must have the supreme place, God comes first in all things. So Shadrach, Meshach and Abed-nego obey Nebuchadnezzar fully and completely until his commandments cross the commandments of God and then, of course, these young men obeyed God, not Nebuchadnezzar. They say to use the language of the New Testament, "we are bound to obey God rather than man". God must have the pre-eminence. The Lord desires us to obey principalities and powers fully and completely, but, if the commandments of our country run counter to the commandments of God, if the laws of our country should tell us to do things that are contrary to God's Word, that, of course, we cannot do. Happy we are in Britain, that, as far as I know, in every respect the laws of our country do not

CHAPTERS 3 & 4

compel us to do anything that is contrary to God. If ever the day should come, and it may if the Lord tarries, when the laws of our country should seek to compel us to do things that are disobedient to God, then God must have the first place. Shadrach, Meshach and Abed-nego say "our God is able to deliver", but if He doesn't see fit to deliver, nevertheless we will honour God; we will seek to obey Him.

These three faithful men are cast into the fiery furnace. Beloved, that brings to our minds I Peter chapter 4. Peter says "Beloved, think it not strange concerning the fiery trial which is to try you". You and I are called upon to go through trials just as Shadrach, Meshach and Abed-nego went through the fire of the furnace. Think it not strange concerning the fiery trial which is to try you. None of us has ever suffered like those three Hebrew young men; it may be that none of us will ever be called upon to suffer like them, but we all in a measure have to pass through the refining fire of the discipline of God. This incident raises a great problem. Here were these young men, the previous chapters have proved them most godly, devout and faithful, and yet they are cast into a fiery furnace. Why should it be? You and I often see godly, noble, spiritual children of God suffer fearful suffering, go through terrible affliction and we ask ourselves, why should it be? Why does God do these things? Well, we do not know; we cannot unravel the mysteries of God; we cannot enter the Divine Mind and tell why God does this and why God does that; you and I are only the creatures, God is the mighty Creator, and the finite cannot comprehend the infinite. Thus we cannot unravel the mysteries of suffering, but we can tell from God's Word, some of the objects of it, some of the purposes for which God allows us to pass through this refining fire. As we look at this experience of Shadrach, Meshach and Abed-nego we shall find at least a seven-fold result of their affliction.

(1) Verse 22,"The furnace exceeding hot, the flame of the fire slew those men that took up Shadrach, Meshach and

DANIEL

Abed-nego". The first thing about these men was that, the fire they went through **destroyed their enemies:** God allows us to go through the fire of affliction that our enemies might be destroyed. We have enemies, pride, selfishness, self desire, evil, deceit, uncleanness, worldliness and carnality, all these are our enemies. God allows the fire of affliction that the discipline of God might remove from us things that are contrary to us. These enemies of the three young men were the mightiest men in Nebuchadnezzar's army, far too strong for them, our enemies, sin in all its forms are far too strong for us, enemies beyond our might, but God allows us to go through the refining fire that these enemies of ours might be destroyed.

(II) The next result was that **it brought them low,** verse 23. "And these three men, Shadrach, Meshach and Abed-nego, fell down bound into the midst of the burning fiery furnace". It brought them low, they fell down. God allows you and me to go through the fire of affliction that it might bring us low. In times of tribulation we realize our own helplessness. You have sometimes stood by the bed of a loved one who is sick and you have felt so utterly helpless; you just long to deliver them and you cannot, you are absolutely helpless. We are sometimes brought into illness ourselves, unable to get up; and with a sense of absolute helplessness, or sometimes we are allowed to enter into circumstances from which no effort of our own can extricate us and there comes that realization of our own impotence. Just as Shadrach, Meshach and Abed-nego were brought down so God allows you and me to go through the refining fire that we might learn lowliness, that we might learn to be humble. In II Corinthians chapter 7 Paul says, "God, that comforteth those that are cast down, comforted us by the coming of Titus;" and the word 'cast down' means 'brought low'.

Now (III), **it manifested the Lord.** The king said "Did not we cast three men into the furnace"? "Well" he says, "I see four men". God deals with us in chastisement, in correction;

CHAPTERS 3 & 4

God deals with us with the rod of discipline in order that the Lord might be manifest in us, in order that Christ might be seen in us. We think of Paul in II Corinthians 12 on the highest heights, caught up to the third heaven, now in the lowest depths, troubled with a thorn in the flesh, but in the midst of it all God says "My grace is sufficient for thee". God is manifested. We think of Jacob coming over Penuel and halting upon his thigh as the sun shone upon him; God was manifested. Shadrach, Meshach and Abed-nego went into the fiery furnace and the Lord was revealed; the Lord was manifested. The reason of all God's discipline, the reason for all God's chastening is that Christ might be manifested in us, to make Christ more vividly manifest in us than ever He was before. I think of one of the most saintly men I know, a mighty man of God; always a spiritual man from the time of his conversion, but there came a time when that man went through a terrible illness and was near the very gates of death. He came out of that a different man than he had ever been before, there was a Christ-likeness about him far greater than when he went into that sickness, and there is today. The psalmist says "Before I was afflicted I went astray." And so Shadrach, Meshach and Abed-nego go through the fire and the Lord is manifested.

But then, (IV) they have **liberty in association with the Son of God,** see verse 25. "He answered and said, Lo, I see four men loose, walking in the midst of the fire; and they have no hurt, and the form of the fourth is like the Son of God". They have got liberty in association with the Son of God. Now that takes us to the eighth chapter of John, where certain disciples trusted in the Lord and the Lord said "Ye shall know the truth and the truth shall make you free," and then He said, "Whom the Son hath made free, they shall be free indeed". Oh beloved, here is liberty with the Son of God. Shadrach, Meshach and Abed-nego go through the fire and the result is liberty in connection with the Son of God. You say, well, what do you mean by liberty? The Bible speaks of

DANIEL

liberty from the law. Galatians chapter 5 "Stand fast in the liberty wherewith Christ hath made you free." It speaks of freedom from the domination of sin in Romans 8 "The law of the spirit of life in Christ Jesus hath made me free from the law of sin and death." Then it speaks of freedom, shall I say in an ecclesiastical sense, John chapter 11 Lazarus came out of the grave and his head was bound—he could not worship, his hands were bound—he could not work, his feet were bound—he could not walk. The Lord said, "Loose him and let him go", and you know, many of us in our christian life need to have that loosing. We have been saved, and after our salvation have been identified with the systems of men, with the ways of men ecclesiastically, as to gathering. We have not known the mind of God, but God has led us on step by step and we have realized the principles of gathering, that God would have His people gather owning no head but the risen Head in the glory. Gathered as no system of man but as those that are one in the body of Christ, with no distinctive ministry but with every member contributing his quota to the work of the body. Oh, the blessed liberty of entering into the mind of God and gathering simply to God's glory.

This liberty is in connection with the Son of God. The Son of God brings us into the family; we are sons in relation to the Son of God and in the family of God there is liberty. Beloved, how often you and I have had to go through the discipline of God to enable us to enter into liberty with the Son of God. I shall never forget when I was twenty-two I had a long illness, lasting many months. During that time and when I became convalescent I began to think to myself — well, I was brought up in a Christian home; my father and mother came into the Assembly when I was about eleven, and I had been taught the truth of the assembly, but had I accepted those things because my parents taught them to me? Had I accepted them because I heard it or did I know that these things were the Word of God. During those months of my convalescence I remember going over the

CHAPTERS 3 & 4

scriptures and seeking to be established in Divine truth and to know that what I was following was the way and the path of God. And, oh, the blessedness of thus enjoying liberty in association with the Son of God.

(V)Then it resulted in the **conversion of a king,** verse 28; "Then Nebuchadnezzar spake, and said, Blessed be the God of Shadrach, Meshach and Abed-nego, Who hath sent His angel, and delivered His servants that trusted in Him". Here was a heathen king, an idolatrous monarch and by the experience of Shadrach, Meshach and Abed-nego he is converted to God. Oh, the beauty of it. Beloved, sometimes God allows you and me to go through dark valleys, to pass through deep waters; what is it for? Sometimes it is, that we might be a blessing to others. When Paul was passing through tribulation II Corinthians chapter 1, he says "All things are for your sakes—not for my sake—but for your sakes" (I am going through this suffering that I may be able to help you!). "He comforteth us in all our tribulation that we may be able to comfort others." God comforts us, says Paul, that we may be able to comfort others, and God often allows us to go through trying experiences that we may be a means in His hands of pointing others to Christ, or of helping other believers, or of encouraging others in the service of the Lord. So, through the experience of Shadrach, Meshach and Abed-nego the king is turned to God.

Now notice, point (VI), they came out and it says "the fire was not upon them". There was no smell of the fire about them. Sometimes when you and I go through a purging experience we come out and the smell of the fire is upon us; there is a change, perhaps of bitterness, or perhaps of sadness, there is a change. But Shadrach, Meshach and Abed-nego **came out in full dignity.** They were cast in, their hats and their hosen, completely clothed, and they came out completely clothed, in full dignity. Oh, beloved, when you and I go through the trials, God help us to come out in moral dignity with character untarnished. Alas, so often in trial we

72 DANIEL

give way to doubting and fears and, dare I say it, even sometimes rebellion against the will of God, but Shadrach, Meshach and Abed-nego come out in full dignity, their characters untarnished. Again notice how they came out. The hats, that's the top; the hosen, that's the bottom; and God delivers them from the top to the bottom — completely; that is the kind of deliverance that God gives, a complete deliverance.

Then finally, (VII), the result of their affliction was that **they had a great reward;** the last verse reads "And the king promoted Shadrach, Meshach and Abed-nego in the province of Babylon". Beloved, you and I are called to suffer with Christ now, but there is a great reward for us by and by, and "our light affliction" says Paul, II Corinthians chapter 4, "Which is but for a moment worketh for us a far more exceeding and eternal weight of glory". So then, we suffer now, but beyond the veil there is for us an exceeding great reward.

Well now, we have looked at chapter three in its prophetic side and then in its practical side as applied to ourselves; now I want you to turn to chapter 4.

This chapter brings before us, as we have read, **the great tree.** Here we get Nebuchadnezzar's own confession of what he learned in the dealings of God. Notice that he starts off by saying "Peace be multiplied unto you"—What a change Nebuchadnezzar's suffering had wrought in him, this tyrannical king, and he has now become a gentle and gracious man and he says "To all people and languages, peace be unto you". It is the grace that the chastening of God has wrought in him. However, I mention that by the way.

Now, again in chapter 4 we have prophetic principles—here is a mighty man, a man who exalts himself above all the world—now humbled and brought low. In the time of the Great Tribulation, when the church is no longer here, God will take these men we have spoken about—the

CHAPTERS 3 & 4

dragon, the beast (the man of sin), the head of the revived Roman empire, and the false prophet, and God will bring them down. He will take the king of the North (Assyria); He will take the king of the South (Egypt); He will take Gog and Magog (Russia) and He will humble them before Himself, He will humble the mighty ones of the earth and they will be compelled to acknowledge the glory of God. And, when the Lord sets up His millenial kingdom—Isaiah says, in chapter 40—"Every valley shall be exalted and every mountain and hill shall be brought low; He will exalt the lowly and He will debase the high". So we see Nebuchadnezzar humbled before God, speaking of the great principle of the humbling of the kings of the earth that will operate in the time of the Tribulation. Then you notice that he was humbled "until seven times passed over him". Now we are not told how long those seven times were, they might have been days or months, we do not know but "he is humbled until seven times passed over him". That points us to the seven years of the Tribulation when God will work in the kings of the earth to humble them and to bring them down before Himself. At the end of that time we read that the kings of the earth shall bring their increase into Jerusalem. Humbled by the hand of God, they will come in lowly subjection, and they will honour the sovereignty of the Lord Jesus Christ. (The Beast and the false prophet will by then, of course, be in the lake of fire). So in Nebuchadnezzar seeking to exalt himself and then being brought low and acknowledging God, we have a picture of the divine working in the time of Tribulation, and in the seven times when he ate straw like an ox we have a picture of those seven years of that period so strongly marked out in Scripture.

Again, we find in chapter four that there are certain vital moral lessons for us. From verse 1 down to verse 27 we have the **watcher** from heaven, in verses 28 to 33 we have the **word** from heaven, in verses 34 to 36 we have the **ways** of heaven, and, then, in verse 37 we have the **worship** ascending up to

74

DANIEL

heaven. Verses 1-27; the watcher from heaven. Nebuchadnezzar had dreamed a dream and there was a great tree in the midst of the earth, the very centre of admiration, and its branches spread everywhere and the beasts came and sheltered under its branches and the birds lodged in the boughs. A great mighty tree, yes, but there came down a watcher from heaven; notice the words of Nebuchadnezzar (verse 13) "I saw in the vision of my head upon my bed and behold a watcher and a holy one came down from heaven". Oh, beloved, a great tree, a prosperous tree, richly endowed, highly favoured, magnificent to behold, stately and resplendent in all its glory, but, there is a watcher from heaven.

Child of God, you and I have been wonderfully blessed. Nebuchadnezzar was blessed materially. You and I have been blessed spiritually; we have been blessed with all spiritual blessings in heavenly places in Christ Jesus, endowed with wealth far beyond Nebuchadnezzar, but, you know in these days you and I are being blessed materially also. These are days of great prosperity in our land and most of us are enjoying some of the benefits of the prosperity of these times, but listen, there is a watcher from heaven. A watcher comes down from heaven and he watches to see how Nebuchadnezzar reacts to the blessings of God. God is watching you and me; He is watching our lives to see how we reciprocate the divine favours, to see how our lives flow out in response to the kindness of God. Beloved, God has so wonderfully blessed us: are we living to show our gratitude, living to show by our lives the depth of our love to Christ, living to show by our obedience to Him our great appreciation of His wonderful love? Remember, God is watching us. "Known unto Thee are all my ways", the psalmist says, "There is not a thought in my heart, but O Lord, Thou knowest it altogether". "Thou knowest my downsitting and mine uprising, Thou knowest my thoughts afar off", and oh fellow believers, dare I say, lovingly and

CHAPTERS 3 & 4

kindly, so many of us are rejoicing in God's wonderful favours, but there is very little return to God, if any at all. In fact in times of prosperity and advantage so many of us have forgotten God. Well, there is a watcher from heaven. You and I, thank God, can never be lost; we can never go into punishment beyond this life, but, oh brethren, there are rewards at the judgment seat of Christ and if our lives are not faithful, well, what a loss there will be. How much we will lose of that great reward. Saved, yes, but losers of the wonderful rewards that God gives to us. Now I have heard Christians say, "Well, I'm not concerned with the reward, I'll be content just as long as I get into heaven", but, oh, child of God, that will not do. God has given you and me a wonderful salvation, yes, but, He does not want us to stop at that. He wants us (as He says in Hebrews) to have respect unto the recompense of the reward. He wants us to go in for that reward. Now there is a watcher from heaven watching every detail of your life and mine.

Secondly, I want you to notice the **word** from heaven in verse 28—"All this came upon king Nebuchadnezzar. At the end of twelve months he walked in the palace of the kingdom of Babylon. The king spoke and said 'Is not this great Babylon, that I have built for the house of the kingdom by the might of my power, and for the honour of my majesty?'". While the word was in the king's mouth, there fell a voice from heaven, saying, "O King Nebuchadnezzar, to thee it is spoken; Thy kingdom is departed from thee". He went out, he looked at his palace, he looked at his city, he looked at his kingdom and he says, "Is not this great Babylon that I have built", and he takes the glory of all his riches to himself. Can it be so with you and me that **we** take to ourselves the glory of what is ours in Christ. Oh, it is so easy in the Christian life to give way to that seductive pride and be living to our own self-advancement instead of to God's praise and glory.

A little while ago I was with a servant of the Lord, a man who ministered the Word much, and during the time I was

76   DANIEL

with him he told me about all his wonderful ministry, how clever he was, how gifted he was, what grand addresses he could give, Oh, child of God, may God save us from that. We are but vessels for His praise, but servants for the honour of Christ; God save us from ever seeking to rob God of the glory that is due to His name.

Well, Nebuchadnezzar says "this is great Babylon that I have built". No, Nebuchadnezzar, it is the Babylon that God has given you, it is the effulgence of His lovingkindness but instead of looking at God's glory you are looking at your own self-advancement. (Beloved how easy it is to be filled with thoughts of our own glory and forget the glory of God). As he says that there comes a voice from Heaven; Heaven's word in the life of Nebuchadnezzar. The word is to tell him he is going to be changed like unto a beast, and for seven times he is going to be driven out into the fields, from the habitation of men, and his nails will grow long like the talons of eagles and his beard will grow long. He will wallow on the ground and eat grass like an ox. Why was that? Nebuchadnezzar is going to be made outwardly what he is inwardly. Inwardly Nebuchadnezzar was just a beast; a beast has no idea of God; a beast lives for food, and perhaps enjoyment, and so on, but it has no idea of God. Nebuchadnezzar lives just like that. There is a spirit in man, the breath of the Almighty to give him understanding. God made us spirit, soul and body that our spirit might have communion with God, but Nebuchadnezzar is living like a beast; God has no place in his life and he is occupied only with material things. So because Nebuchadnezzar is inwardly like a beast God is going to make him outwardly so, and he will grovel in the grass like a beast of the field. Beloved, in the Christian life, you and I become outwardly what we are inwardly. Remember that the thoughts and emotions in your heart and mine, sooner or later show themselves. If we are dwelling in carnality, we will become carnal christians; if we are living for material gain we will

CHAPTERS 3 & 4

become materialistic christians; if we are dwelling in pride we will become proud and haughty christians and sooner or later these things will evidence themselves in our lives. Nebuchadnezzar had been living like a beast: the people of his kingdom did not know that, they thought what a splendid fellow he was. It is going to be manifest. Beloved, what you and I are living inwardly, what you and I are thinking inwardly, sooner or later will be manifest in us. Saith the Scripture, "As a man thinketh in his heart so is he". Seven times passed over Nebuchadnezzar.

But now, I want you to think of the **ways of heaven,** verse 34. "And at the end of the days I, Nebuchadnezzar, lifted up mine eyes unto heaven and mine understanding returned unto me, and I blessed the Most High, and I praised and honoured Him that liveth for ever, Whose dominion is an everlasting dominion, and His kingdom is from generation to generation. And all the inhabitants of the earth are reputed as nothing, and He doeth according to His will in the army of heaven, and among the inhabitants of the earth." In verses 28-33 Nebuchadnezzar had looked up **to his kingdom,** in verses 34-37 he looks up to **God's kingdom.** In verses 28-33 he looked at Babylon; in verses 34-37 he looks up to heaven. He is a wise man at last. The vision is no longer filled with self but he is gazing up to glory. He says, "I looked unto heaven". Then as he looks up to heaven he learns the ways of God; what about his glory now? He has no time to bother with that, no time to think of his own glory; "I lifted up my voice and I blessed Him that liveth for ever and ever, His dominion is an everlasting dominion." He saw that though he was the head of gold that very soon the shoulders of silver would follow and then the belly of brass and the legs of iron. He recognises that his glory is a transient thing but that God's dominion is an everlasting dominion.

So he turns from his passing dominion to the eternal glory of the King of Kings; he is occupied with God's eternal dominion. Yes, and he speaks of the ways of heaven; "He

78 DANIEL

doeth according to his will among the armies of heaven and the hosts of earth". "We", says Nebuchadnezzar in effect, "kings though we are, we are mere puppets, mere grasshoppers". "We are as but the dust of the earth in His sight and He takes us up and does according to His will amongst us and He works out His own purposes and none can stay His hand nor say unto Him, what doest thou?" Nebuchadnezzar is filled with the conception of the glory of God. Notice God's reaction to this. Nebuchadnezzar has now got the thoughts of a man: God made man for His own glory, and now Nebuchadnezzar has glorified God. Because he has the true thoughts of a man God lifts him to manhood; Nebuchadnezzar is raised up and the tangled growth upon his face disappears, his talons go, his flowing spittle abates, he ceases to eat of the grass; he is a man at last, what he is inwardly be becomes outwardly. When he thought like a beast God made him like a beast, now he thinks like a man God makes him like a man. Oh beloved, our thoughts are going to mould and shape our lives. If we are thinking beastly thoughts, (forgive me using rough and crude words) we shall be bestial men and women, but on the other hand, if we are thinking manly thoughts we will be manly men and women. What are manly thoughts? They are thoughts of God and God's glory, for the whole purpose for which God made man was that man might glorify Him. What kind of people are we, beastly people or manly people? It will show itself. "As a man thinketh in his heart so is he." So Nebuchadnezzar learns the ways of heaven.

Finally, there is the **worship ascending to heaven.** "Now I Nebuchadnezzar praise and extol the King of heaven, all whose works are truth and His ways judgment; and those that walk in pride He is able to abase". Now he had got right with God, and there is worship ascending to heaven and that changed and transformed a man who for so long has worshipped himself, but now worships the living and Almighty God. Oh, child of God, that this may be true of you

CHAPTERS 3 & 4

and me. "Oh worship the King all glorious above." God grant that, filled with a sense of the grandeur and beauty and splendour of our Lord Jesus Christ, our whole lives may be lived to His praise. So we read here concerning Nebuchadnezzar of the **Watcher** from heaven, of the **Word** from heaven, of the **Ways** of heaven and of the **Worship ascending** to heaven.

May God help us that these things may be a blessing to us all.

Daniel Chapters 5 & 6

Mr. Bell read from Daniel chapter 5 verses 1 to 3, verses 5 and 6, verse 13, verses 25 to 31. Chapter 6 verses 1 and 2, verses 4 and 5, verses 10 and 11 and verses 16 to 22.

You will remember we considered previously that the historical chapters of the book of Daniel recount things that have happened in the past; we have prophetic principles; principles that shall work out in a day that is yet to come when the Church is home with the Lord. In chapters 5 and 6 we have two elements; **corruption** in chapter 5 and **violence** in chapter 6. In the book of the Revelation also, when the church has gone to be with Christ, we find those two elements outstanding. There is the Beast — the man of sin, the head of the revived Roman empire; in him we see **violence**. Then there is in Revelation 17 a woman who is "Babylon the great, the mother of harlots," — false Christianity, Satan's counterfeit, notably Roman Catholicism, the blasphemous counterfeit of the true church that belongs to Christ; and in her we see **corruption**. So there is corruption in the woman and violence in the Beast and those two elements persist right throughout the Word of God. If we go back to Genesis chapter 6 God says that the wickedness of man was great in the earth—that is violence, and every imagination of his heart was only evil continually — that is corruption. Daniel chapters 5 and 6 show us the character of those final days, corruption in chapter 5 and violence in chapter 6. In chapter 5 we have the **writing of God;** God with His hand writes on the wall of Belshazzar's palace. In chapter 6 we have the **writing of the king;** the writing of king Darius who wrote a commandment and confirmed it with his own hand, that for thirty days nobody

82

DANIEL

should make request of God or man, save of him. Now the writing in chapter 5 (the writing of God) was irreversible, nothing could alter it, for there is with God no shadow of turning; "God is not a man that He should lie, neither the son of man that He should repent". Then in chapter 6 there is the writing of king Darius, and God stepped in regarding that writing, that seemingly unalterable decree, and reversed it altogether and saved Daniel alive. Thus in chapter 5 we have Babylonish corruption, Belshazzar in Babylon is having a gluttonous feast, he brings the holy vessels of God, and blasphemes God. Now Babylon in the scripture stands for the world religiously, and Babylon is taken to be a picture of the false church — Satan's counterfeit — Satan's duplication, Satan's worthless, spurious imitation of the church that belongs to Christ (notably what we have in Roman Catholicism).

Throughout the Scriptures when God wants to show us corrupt religion He takes up the figure of a woman. In Kings and Chronicles we have Jezebel and Atholiah, wicked women who sought to bring religious evil into Israel; in the book of Proverbs chapter 9 we have the foolish woman, who is clamourous and knoweth nothing, seeking to delude people who are right in their way, and God says of her that her guests are in the depths of hell. In Zechariah chapter 5 we have those two women with the ephah who bring uncleanness into Israel and God sends them away to Babylon where they rightly belong. When we turn to the New Testament, in Matthew chapter 13 the Kingdom of Heaven is like unto leaven which a woman hid in three measures of meal until the whole is leavened; here is the woman of ecclesiastical wickedness. Then in Revelation chapter 17 we find her in full bloom; there is a woman who sits on seven hills, drunken with the blood of martyrs and her name is Babylon the great, the mother of harlots. Babylon, and especially this Babylonish woman stands for Satan's counterfeit of christianity. We mentioned earlier that the

CHAPTERS 5 & 6

devil will have in those days his counterfeit of the Trinity, the dragon, the beast and the false prophet, duplicating the Father, the Son and the Holy Spirit and then as a counterfeit of Christ and the church we will have the beast and the woman riding on the beast.

So Daniel chapter 5 in figure gives the picture of that spirit of religious corruption which is wholly opposed to God. People might have stood and looked at Belshazzar's feast and thought how grand it was as they saw the lords in their splendour and the ladies in their finery, the wine poured out, the splendour of the furnishings; all so magnificent. God says it is rotten at the very core. All is utterly opposed to God, and God denounces the thing in its totality, root and branch; the whole as contrary to Himself, a monstrous idolatrous thing. In christendom today we see a system with vestments, incense, altars, penances, confessionals, purgatorial teaching and all that sort of thing; well it is Satan's counterfeit of the Church that belongs to Christ and God says it is utterly base, utterly vile, utterly corrupt. God says "Come out from them my people, that ye be not contaminated with a plague". Well, that is God's judgment of the world's church, the devil's counterfeit of the church that belongs to Christ. That is the principle that comes out in chapter 5.

In chapter 6 we get another principle, that of **violence;** the violence of the beast in the time of the Great Tribulation. Daniel is faithful to God, he relies upon God, he will not be swayed by the wiles of men and consequently he has got to go through the den of lions. Now the lion stands for kingship; the lion is the monarch of the beasts. Well, here is Daniel in the den of lions, pointing to that day when the godly remnant out of Israel and the saved ones from among the Gentiles (saved under the Gospel of the Kingdom when the church has gone) will suffer affliction at the hands of the kings of the earth in rebellion against God. In that day, the remnant of God's people from the Jews and from the Gentiles will suffer

84 DANIEL

terrible affliction at the hands of the kings of the earth who are opposed to God and against His Christ. Some of them will be slain in the tribulation and their souls are under the altar crying unto God for vengeance.

Then in Revelation chapter 7 we have one hundred and forty four thousand out of Israel and a multitude out of the Gentiles who are preserved alive through the Tribulation to be the nucleus of the millenial earth. Well, Daniel chapter 6 is a picture of that, a picture of the persecutions of God's people at the hands of the kings of the earth in that day. By way of illustration, of what I mean when speaking of the den of lions representing the kings of the earth; you will remember when the apostle Paul was on trial before Nero in 2 Timothy chapter 4 he says "The Lord stood with me and I was delivered out of the mouth of the lion," referring to Nero. So in that coming day, in the Tribulation, the rulers of the earth are characterized as lions, and God's people of that day (not the church of course, for the church will be at home), will have to contend with the lions in their witness to Christ because they refuse to bow to the mark of the Beast, because they embrace the message of the Kingdom and because they are prepared to welcome the coming Messiah. That is the time of which God's Word says "They that endure to the end shall be saved", those that endure to the end of the Tribulation, receiving the gospel of the Kingdom and refusing the mark of the Beast; they will be saved out of it to form the nucleus of God's people on earth. So in these chapters, we have the two great evil principles of the tribulation: corruption in chapter 5 and violence in chapter 6.

Chapter 5 has certain very precious moral lessons to impart to us.

In verses 1 to 4 we have Belshazzar's *feast*.

In verses 5 to 12 we have Belshazzar's *fear*.

In verses 12 to 28 we have Belshazzar's *failure*.

CHAPTERS 5 & 6

In verses 29 to 32 we have Belshazzar's *favour*

Verses 1-4 Belshazzar's feast. Belshazzar the king made a feast unto a thousand of his lords and he called for the holy vessels from the temple of God. In Belshazzar, this wicked king of Babylon, we see insensibility to God. (Just as Romans chapter 1 speaks of certain who are past feeling and Paul writing to Timothy of those who have their consciences seared with a red hot iron). When I loved the things of the world, occasionally there used to come to Jarrow where I lived, a fair, and as a worldly boy, I used to go wandering into the fair. I remember there used to be a performance that always thrilled me. There were some African men who had a great fire, with red hot irons in the fire, and they would bring out the red hot irons and walk over them in their bare feet and I used to be thrilled at the performance of these men. Well, I suppose the secret of it, in part anyway, was that they gradually allowed themselves to become hardened to it. They could walk over red hot irons without getting hurt because their feet had become cauterized. Well, that is the condition of Belshazzar; he was insensible to the things of God, insensible to God's judgment. At that time Belshazzar is at war with Darius the king of the Medes and Persians, and the armies of Darius are at his very doors; the judgment of God is upon him and he is so sodden with sin, so saturated with iniquity that he is feasting, indifferent to the fact that the very judgment of God is at his gate. Again, he is insensible to all the lessons of the past.

We saw in chapter 4 what God had done to Belshazzar's grandfather Nebuchadnezzar. He knows how God humbled his grandfather and yet these lessons make no impression upon him and he stoops to sinful acts that his grandfather never committed. Nebuchadnezzar never took the holy vessels to drink from, but Belshazzar does, going far beyond any of the degradations of his grandfather, insensible to the lesssons of the past. Again, he is insensible to the prophetic word. Where is Daniel? Daniel is not in it; he knows nothing

86 DANIEL

about Daniel. Daniel is dismissed out of his kingdom altogether. Now when his grandfather was on the throne Daniel was his right hand man, but here is Belshazzar with no room for Daniel. Insensible to the judgment of God, insensible to the lessons of the past, insensible to the prophetic word and then insensible to the holiness of God, he does not tremble, or even shudder as they bring those holy vessels from the temple into his presence. Belshazzar, going in for feasting becomes insensible to the things of God, a very, very solemn lesson for you and me.

Fellow-believers, worldlinesss in a christian, worldly occupation, becoming engrossed in wordly things, going in for the transient things of this world produces dullness of spiritual feeling, insensibility to the things of God, a lack of appreciation of Divine things. In our meetings today one often meets people who once were bright for God but the world has come into their lives and they have drifted worldward, and, while still coming to the meetings, still orthodox and all that sort of thing, dare I say it, they have lost their appreciation of Christ and the old finer spiritual feelings that once characterized them, they have lost their appreciation of the things of God. Worldliness dulls the spiritual apprehension. Furthermore, if God reveals truth to you and me, if God reveals His mind to us through the Word, and we resist that revelation, it will always lead to dullness of spiritual apprehension. There is nothing so deadening to the spiritual faculties as the resisting of His Word. God help us, that we may be truly separate, and that our hearts may be yielded to God's Word so that nothing will dull our spiritual sensitivity. May we have a consciousness of the holiness of God; of the truth of His Word, of the guidance of the Spirit and not dullness of hearing, or dullness of seeing.

So then we find Belshazzar insensible to the judgment of God, insensible to the lessons of the past, insensible to the prophetic word and insensible to the holiness of God.

We pass on to think now (verses 5-12) of Belshazzar's fear.

CHAPTERS 5 & 6

Suddenly, in the midst of all this jollification there comes a hand upon the wall, writing on the plaster; Mene, Mene, Tekel, Upharsin; — Oh — the terribleness of it. The wall in scripture is sometimes used as a symbol of the record of a man's life. When Hezekiah was sick and Isaiah told him he must die, it says, "he turned his face to the wall", a picture of shame as it were, surveying his life before him. As a corrective in their ways God told the Israelites to put texts in the walls of their houses. Well, there is a hand writing on the wall, it is God's verdict, God's assessment of the life of Belshazzar, God's judgment of that man. Now Belshazzar although insensible to everything else could not be insensible to the judgment of God. "Who shall stand in the day of His wrath." Who shall resist the judgment of God? Thank God that you and I are saved through faith in our Lord Jesus Christ, but may I pause and ask this; is it possible that my words are reaching somebody who is not a Christian, who has never been born again. Dear friend, give this your utmost attention — have you taken the warning of the judgment of God? Belshazzar, who never trembled at anything else, trembled when he saw the handwriting of God's judgment. Unsaved one, the wicked shall be turned into hell: God says, "He that believeth not the Son shall not see life but the wrath of God abideth on him." There is eternal wrath, eternal torment in hell for the soul that dies without Christ and, oh, dear unsaved person, if such there be reached by these words, what a grand thing it would be if in these Bible readings you did what Belshazzar did not do, and you turned and repented and trusted the Saviour. The Scripture says that "God so loved the world that He gave His only begotten Son", (gave Him to die in your stead), "that whosoever believeth in Him should not perish but have everlasting life!"

So there, before this startled man there comes this terrible fear of the wrath and judgment of God, and as a result, and because of the queen's intervention in verse 13, we have

88 DANIEL

Daniel brought before Belshazzar and he outlines Belshazzar's failure. By the way, I should mention in connection with the bringing in of Daniel, the commendation he received, first of Belshazzar's wife who said that "the spirit of the holy gods was in Daniel, and further that there was a wisdom in him like the holy gods", and Belshazzar himself said that "an excellent spirit was found in him." Now, here is Daniel, the spirit of God in him; God-likeness in him. The spirit of God in him, that is communion; he was like God, that is conformity, and an excellent spirit was in him, that is character. Oh beloved, God help you and me that moving amid a corrupt world, a degenerate world, a world that is worsening and bound for judgment, we may manifest these noble characteristics of communion, of conformity, of character, that by so doing we may commend the gospel of the Lord Jesus Christ. However, Daniel goes on to tell of Belshazzar's failure. (I should say that the word 'father' in verse 18 can be rendered either father or grandfather. In our English versions it is rendered 'father' but can equally mean grandfather and historicaly it would appear that Belshazzar was the son of Nabonidus who was the son of Nebuchadnezzar, so that Belshazzar was the grandson of Nebuchadnezzar. It would seem the supreme king was Nabonidus his father, and Belshazzar reigned as a kind of regent or viceroy for his father, so consequently, he says to Daniel that he would promote him to the **third** man in the kingdom. Nabonidus was the first man, Belshazzar the second man and Daniel became the third man. However, I mention that by the way).

Daniel told Belshazzar that his father (or grandfather) Nebuchadnezzar was richly blessed of God. God had given him abundant riches, abundant territory, abundant increase; God showered His favours upon him, but, when he forgot God, God turned him into the likeness of an ox, until he looked up and gave God glory. Daniel warned Belshazzar

CHAPTERS 5 & 6   89

that he was not like his grandfather Nebuchadnezzar who repented and turned to God, for Belshazzar had received many warnings but had gone on in continued rebellion against God with no sign of repentance. Thus he warns Belshazzar of his terrible failure. Now, beloved, when we come to that point we can notice two things that mark the condition of this man. When God spoke to Nebuchadnezzar, it was through dreams as we read in chapter 2 and chapter 4 but when God spoke to Belshazzar it is no dream but handwriting on the wall: why is that? There was something in Nebuchadnezzar that God could work on; there was a consciousness in the man, and in some measure he had a regard for God and so God could influence his mind by these dreams, but in Belshazzar there was nothing God could work on, a man so utterly hardened against God. God could not speak to him in a dream, so God speaks externally, objectively, outside the man altogether and a hand writes upon the wall. Then again, Daniel spoke to Belshazzar as he never did to Nebuchadnezzar. For when Belshazzar offered him great gifts, Daniel says "thy gifts be to another". The sacrifice of the wicked is an abomination in the sight of God, and Daniel recoils at the thought of Belshazzar's corrupt gift. Such is the awful failure of this dreadful man in those days of long ago.

We have thought of Belshazzar's *feast*, of Belshazzar's *fear* and of Belshazzar's *failure*; before we leave it let us look at the writing, Mene, Mene, Tekel, Upharsin. "Mene" says Daniel, "God hath numbered thy kingdom and finished it." Tekel — "thou art weighed in the balances and art found wanting." Upharsin — "thy kingdom is divided and taken from thee and given to the Medes and Persians." God says three things about Belshazzar; his time, himself, and his kingdom. **His time—**"God hath numbered thy kingdom and finished it." His time was numbered, very soon he is going to come under the judgment of God. **Himself—**"thou art weighed in the balances and found wanting." **His**

90   DANIEL

kingdom—"thy kingdom is divided and given unto the Medes and Persians." This is a picture of how God will judge at the Great Tribulation, judge the kings of the world who rejected God, who spurned God's Christ, who murdered and slew His people, who built an image and blasphemed God's holy name; it is a picture of the judgment of God that will fall upon the earth in the time of the Great Tribulation.

Then, last of all, we read of Belshazzar's favour, verse 29 "Then commanded Belshazzar and they clothed Daniel in scarlet and put a chain of gold about his neck and made a proclamation concerning him that he should be the third ruler in the kingdom. There was no sign of repentance towards God, yet, God made His servant Daniel triumph over all opposition and, in spite of all the hostility of Belshazzar, Daniel becomes the third ruler in the kingdom. Beloved, as you and I go through this world seeking to live for Christ, we encounter opposition and hostility but nothing can mar the purposes of God. Daniel, in spite of it all, is the third ruler in the kingdom and, however great the world's hostility towards us, nothing can rob us of that glory, that prospect, that blessing, that privilege, that eternal splendour that is ours in the purposes of God. Now, the story ends like this: Belshazzar passed away, Daniel remained in blessing. It is the age old story; men who raise themselves up in opposition to God and His word, men who trample under foot the Son of God, men who refuse the Gospel of Christ, like Belshazzar, will wax and will wane, they will fade and they will die; just as Belshazzar goes and Daniel remains in blessing.

While God's enemies will perish and suffer eternally the judgment of God, those who believe in Christ as Saviour, those who are faithful to Him, those who walk with Christ, shall endlessly share the blessing and the love of God. You and I have seen it in our own days. We have seen men like Hitler and Stalin, wicked men who hurled themselves in opposition to God, who blasphemed God's holy name, who

CHAPTERS 5 & 6   91

denied the Gospel, who refused the very message of Christianity and who persecuted the people of God, and they have all gone, and yet God is still leading on His people, leading them through this wilderness to that home where they will ever abide with Himself. Belshazzar goes, Daniel remains; the kings of this world go but they that love their God are stable as Mount Zion, settled and blessed forever. Thus we have the truth of chapter 5, grim, solemn and startling and yet not without its side of comfort and blessing for God's people. Let us remember then, Belshazzar's *feast*, Belshazzar's *fear*, Belshazzar's *failure*, and Belshazzar's *favour* that he heaped upon Daniel by the sovereign control of God.

Now, look with me at chapter 6. Verses 1-9 — Daniel in his *public life*. Verses 10-15 — Daniel in his *private life*. Verses 16 to the end of the chapter — Daniel in his *personal life*. In verses 1-9 we have Daniel as an officer, a governor of the province of Babylon — Daniel's public life. In verses 10-15 we have Daniel at home, a picture of his private life. Then in verses 16 to the end of the chapter we have a more intimate picture still; Daniel in his personal life, alone in the lions' den. Beloved, you and I have three phases of our life: even four if you care to go into it in detail, but three phases in particular. We have our public life, the life that we live before men; we have our private life—the life that we live in our home; we have our personal life—the life that we live solely before God when nobody else is near.

In Daniel's public life we see purity; the lords of king Darius tried to find fault with Daniel in his administration of the affairs of Babylon, and they found absolutely nothing — purity in his public life. In Daniel's private life we find prayer; when Daniel heard of the edict that had gone forth against him he went home and prayed — prayer was the characteristic of his private life. In Daniel's personal life we find patience; all night he is in the den of lions, but there

92 DANIEL

unwavering and unweary he continues, patient through the hours of the night.

"It pleased Darius to set over the kingdom an hundred and twenty princes which should be over the whole kingdom; and over these three presidents of whom Daniel was the first: that the princes might give accounts unto them and the king should have no damage." Now, here is a man who is put into a place of dizzy eminence, the absolute ruler of Babylon next to Darius, a place fraught with tremendous danger, is it not? I wonder if I am addressing myself to young ones who are being advanced in their occupation: God has prospered you and you are climbing to the heights in your particular occupation; dear young brethren and sisters, be careful, there are perils attached to promotion and as you advance from step to step in the occupation that you follow, remember that every step higher brings greater dangers. Yet, if it is God's will that you should advance like that, remember this, you have a great God who will keep you in that high position, but, child of God, it will mean diligently seeking Him and constant communion; it will mean continuous walking with Christ lest in that high position you should stumble and fall. In my life as a christian I have known, alas, a number of christians who attained high position, and then they slipped and had terrible falls because they were not walking in constant communion with God. Oh, young brother, young sister, if you are being prospered in your work, keep close to the Lord, cling to Him with all your might; never neglect that daily prayer and reading of the Word and that daily fellowship with Christ, never neglect the things of the Assembly, the gathering together of God's people, for if you do, I tell you it will be a terrible fall. However, here is Daniel in this position. Now the lords of Babylon plotted against him and sought to find fault against him so that they could accuse him to the king. They spied on Daniel; they pried into all his work; they watched him, but they could not find a fault. Here is Daniel, flawless in his

CHAPTERS 5 & 6

service for the king. Oh, child of God, may God make you and me conscientious, industrious men and women in our daily labours. You know, I am not in an earthly occupation now but I am conscious from what I hear that there is a great deal of slack working today; there is a great deal of carelessness in the daily occupations of men and women: God grant that that may never be laid to your door and mine as Christians. God give us diligence in our earthly occupations: the Scripture says, "Not slothful in business, fervent in spirit, serving the Lord". Paul says to the Colossians about serving our earthly masters, "Not with eye service as men pleasers". May God give us purity in our workaday life, and if any of us here are in business on our own account, may I speak to you earnestly: there is such a temptation in business to indulge in shady practices, dishonest things: God help us as Christians never to be contaminated or tarnished by shady practices in our business life: may God keep us ever from that. So then in Daniel there was purity in his public life.

From verse 10 we find Daniel in his private life; he goes home. I am only going to touch upon this at the moment and return to it afterwards but we read that when Daniel heard of the edict that went forth, he went home, and there in his home he prayed three times a day to God. Beloved, Daniel had a heavenly, a spiritual home, a home life enveloped in prayer. May I gently ask, fellow believers, what kind of a home have you got? Oh, you know the question of the christian's home life is so formidable in these days. Many a christian home is being contaminated and defiled and consequently the service for the Lord is weakened, debilitated, stunted, withered. Is our home a place where husband and wife are angry with each other, where they give way to quarelling and bickering, a home where the wife takes a delight in criticizing her husband, the husband a delight in being cynical and unkind to his wife, where the children are undisciplined, where they are neglected, where they are not

94   DANIEL

corrected and not taught in the Word of God, and where the children are allowed to dominate the parents? Is it a home where worldliness comes in: I say this lovingly and kindly; is it a home where the family spend hours glued around the television occupied with the world, or where they spend their time in reading the filthy things in the newspapers or the questionable attraction of modern novels? Oh, beloved, God grant that our homes may be like the home of Daniel, homes of Christlike purity, homes that breathe the atmosphere of heaven. I do not mean to put it harshly, but it is such an urgent necessity in the Christian life today. As I go up and down the country I find that so many Christians are being defiled at home, and you know, the amazing thing to me is this that I have visited homes where they are very keen and zealous about discipline and order in the Assembly, a most essential thing, but, they have none in their own homes. These things are true fellow believers, and we would do well to think about them.

Then we have Daniel in his personal life, Daniel cast into the den of lions. That night king Darius could not sleep but I am quite sure that Daniel slept. That night king Darius had no music, for it was the custom for the musicians to gather in his private chamber and play to him so that slumber would be induced. Ah! but Daniel had music; he had in his heart the music of the melody of God; he heard, as it were, if I may borrow a New Testament scripture, "I will never leave thee nor forsake thee", he heard God saying as He said to Jacob and to Joshua, "Certainly I will be with thee". King Darius had no rest but Daniel is resting on the bosom of God. All through the night king Darius tossed upon his bed and Daniel rested calmly in the den of lions, confident in God. Now, beloved it is an emergency, a crisis, that brings out what we are. D.L. Moody said, character is what a man does when he is in the dark, character is what a man is when he is alone. In Scotland they have a saying about the difference between character and reputation. They say of a fruiterer

CHAPTERS 5 & 6 95

who has a barrel of apples at his shop door, that his reputation is at the top of the barrel, but his character is at the bottom. Beloved, character is what you and I are in the secrets of our own hearts. So there is Daniel in the den of lions with nobody to see him, it is Daniel alone; no question of keeping up appearances now, it is Daniel's own character that comes out in the den of lions and there he is a man that has trust and confidence in God. Although I was very young I never forget hearing the late Mr. Henry Pickering touch upon this one night. He was speaking on Romans 8 and he just happened to mention Daniel and he spoke of how there were three kings there, the king of beasts—the lion, the king of Medo-Persia—Darius, and the King of Kings was there looking after Daniel, and, said Mr. Pickering, "All through the night the king of beasts, the lion, was coming near to Daniel and saying, 'Yes its all right for you Daniel, you've got a protector, but woe betide the next man who comes in here' ". Well, Daniel was protected by the power of God. Oh, beloved, may God give you and me that personal, private, individual character, strong in the Lord and in the power of His might. So we have seen Daniel in his public life — purity. Daniel in his private life — prayer. Daniel in his personal life — patience.

Now, as a kind of footnote I want to go back to verse 10 where we read about Daniel's prayer life. "Now whcn Daniel knew that the writing was signed he went into his house." Here is Daniel's approach to prayer; he knew that the writing was signed against him and so he approached his house to resort to prayer. When difficulties arise, God grant that they may drive you and me to prayer. When this difficulty approaches Daniel, he goes home that he might pray; his circumstances constrain him to pray. First then we have his **approach** to prayer. Then we have the **atmosphere** of prayer, his windows being opened. Beloved, when Daniel prayed he had nothing between himself and God, not even the thickness of a window pane, and that speaks of the

96   DANIEL

atmosphere of prayer. If you and I pray, having confessed our failures, having confessed our shortcoming, having put things right in our lives, that is the time when we will get answers to our prayers. If you and I pray "with the windows open" as it were, not having even the thickness of a window pane between us and God, no cloud between, then, we will not ask amiss; our prayers will be guided by the Holy Spirit of God.

Then we have the **altitude** of Daniel's prayer. It says he prayed the windows being open **in his chamber.** Now Mr. Darby tells us the word translated "chamber" means literally the "upper chamber". Oh beloved here is the altitude of prayer. Daniel in his prayer soars above the mundane things of earth and is occupied with God in Heaven. God give us that altitude in prayer.

"Lord lift me up and let me stand,
By faith on Heaven's table land,
A higher plane than I have found,
Lord, plant my feet on higher ground."

Oh that you and I might have prayers like this.

Then we read of the **attention** in prayer. He prays towards Jerusalem, Daniel gave attention to the mind of God, but, you may say, "What is the good of praying towards Jerusalem, for it is destroyed and the temple is ruined"; but God put His Name there and God never turns from His purpose, so Daniel attends to the mind of God. "His attention is towards Jerusalem". Now when you and I pray God grant that our attention may be towards heaven, the heavenly Jerusalem, where Christ sits at the right hand of God.

Then we have the **attitude** of prayer "he kneeled upon his knees"; now you know that the kneeling suggests submission and subjection to God's will. Beloved, God always wants in prayer that there may be a yieldedness of the will, "Thy will,

CHAPTERS 5 & 6   97

Lord", "Nevertheless not my will but Thine be done", the attitude of prayer.

Then we have the **apprehension** of prayer, he prayed three times a day, but why three times a day? Daniel had wonderful intelligence and the Spirit of God reveals to him the principle on which Christ in the garden prayed three times, the principle on which Paul in 2 Corinthians chapter 12 prayed three times that the thorn in the flesh might be removed. Now three is the number of the Trinity speaking of prayer to the Father by the power of the Spirit for the Glory of the Son. He prays to God as the Object, the power of the Spirit as the Strength and through the Son as the means, the ground of blessing. Three is the figure of death, burial and resurrection. Then finally fellow believers there is the **acknowledgment** of prayer "and he gave thanks to God." Oh beloved, Daniel in all his prayers acknowledged the blessings of God. God help you and me to be thankful, appreciative of the blessings of God. Then there is one other thing, his **adhesion** to prayer; "as he did aforetime"; here is Daniel going on as he did before. "Daniel, stop praying for thirty days" they said; but not so for Daniel, he will go on, he cannot forsake God for thirty days; he goes on in prayer, there is adhesion to prayer. So in verse 10 we have seen Daniel's *approach* to prayer, when he heard that the writing was signed he went into his house. Then there is the *atmosphere* of prayer—his windows being opened—nothing between. Then there is the *altitude* of prayer—it was the chamber—the upper chamber. Then the *attention* in prayer—he prayed towards Jerusalem, having his eyes towards God. Then the *attitude* of prayer—he kneeled upon his knees, subjection to God. Then the *apprehension* of prayer, apprehension of the Divine mind—three times a day. Then the *acknowledgement* of prayer — giving thanks before his God, and then the *adhesion* to prayer — as he did aforetimes, stedfastly going on, continuing in prayer. Oh beloved, what shall we say to this;

DANIEL

"All earthly things with earth shall fade away,
Prayer grasps eternity, pray, always pray."

Oh may God grant that in your life and mine there may be this steadfast, unceasing, unrelaxing, going on in prayer to God's glory.

Daniel Chapter 7

Mr. Bell read Daniel Chapter 7

We come now to the second part of the book of Daniel. You will remember that we sought to point out in our introduction, that the first six chapters were historical, the latter six prophetical, indicating that in the former six chapters we have prophetic principles, but in the last six chapters the prophetic plan. Hence we are now in the strictly prophetic section, dealing with God's prophetic plan and purpose for this world.

There are two sections; verses 1-14, the vision, and verses 15 to the end, the interpretation of the vision. The second section, where God gives Daniel the interpretation of the vision, adds much to it, and that is characteristic, for whenever we find God interpreting something He always gives more detail than we have in the original account; such is the abundance of the revelation of God. In the first section, we have two sub sections; verses 1-8 we read about four kingdoms that shall arise, and in verses 9-14 about one Kingdom—the Kingdom of God. Verse 1 "In the first year of Belshazzar, king of Babylon". We saw in chapter five that in the reign of Belshazzar there was deterioration. Nebuchadnezzar had begun in magnificence and splendour, but in the reign of Belshazzar things declined and decayed, and you can well imagine Daniel's awareness of this as he witnessed the whole state becoming rotten and corrupt. Then God comes to him in wonderful grace and reveals the whole prospect in the deterioration of the realm. "So in the first year of Belshazzar, Daniel had a dream and visions of his head upon his bed; then he wrote the dream, and told the sum of the matter". Now look to the last verse of the chapter,

99

100 DANIEL

"I kept the matter in my heart". He starts with visions of his head, but by the end of the chapter the thing has worked down to his heart. That is what God always wants with His word. All this prophecy in scripture is not just there to be interesting and to satisfy our curiosity, to charm and fascinate (though it does all these things) but is given that it might reach, stir, and soften our hearts. God wants these things not simply as detail or as truth even, in our heads, but in power to affect our hearts.

Verse 2 "Daniel spake and said, I saw in my vision by night, and behold, the four winds of the heaven strove upon the great sea, and four beasts came up from the sea, diverse one from another". The four beasts are world empires, and they come forth in the appointed time. How do they come forth? By activity in the heavens, for we read the four winds strove upon the great sea; the things which happen upon earth are the result of things which happen in heaven. This is a surprising and solemn thing; we look at the newspapers and read of leading political figures, great men, and all their international moves, but behind all, there are unseen forces at work, the forces of heaven, moving and activating the world rulers whether for good or for bad. In Ephesians 6 we read "We wrestle not against flesh and blood, but against principalities, against powers, against the rulers of the darkness of this world, against spiritual wickedness in high places". The darkness of this world is governed by spiritual forces in heavenly places, in other words by Satan and his hosts. Yet we thank God that He comes in all this satanic scene, where "the whole world lieth in the wicked one" and over-rules, for He has never relinquished His sovereignty and up until now has lengthened out times of peace that we might have liberty to preach the gospel, to live for Christ, and manifest His glory down here. So the political and international activities of earth are the result of unseen forces at work behind it all. That is why it is so important for us to "pray for all men (as we read in I Timothy 2) for kings,

CHAPTER 7   101

and for rulers, and all that are in authority", as we realize the satanic forces that lie behind them.

As to the winds striving upon the great sea, this latter is the Mediterranean Sea, and it is striking how prophecies have their centre there; the Roman empire of the past lay all around it.

The four beasts coming up out of the sea, diverse one from another, represent four world empires. Isaiah 57 tells us that the nations in their confusion, sorrow, distress and perplexity are "like a troubled sea", and this is a fitting description of the scene from which these great empires arise. In the midst of turmoil, national distress and unrest, with peoples looking for a deliverer, these four world emperors rise to the situation, just as, in more modern times, Napoleon emerged out of the whirlpool of trouble in France.

Now "the first was like a lion and had eagle's wings". We need not doubt what these four kingdoms represent for we saw them in chapter two as the head of gold, Babylon; the shoulders of silver, Medo-Persia; the body of brass, Greece; and legs of iron, Rome. Yet here there is a difference; in chapter two we saw them in all their magnificence, an image impressive, terrible, wonderful, as Daniel saw it, but now we have these empires in their inner reality, as God views them, likened unto a ravening lion, a growling bear, a slinking leopard, a monstrous nondescript sort of beast.

The winged lion is the Babylonian empire. The lion is the king of beasts, and Nebuchadnezzar, head of the supreme Babylonian empire, the greatest of the four empires, had absolute authority, a complete unchallenged authority, which none of the succeeding emperors had. The lion "had eagle's wings". The great wings of the eagle can carry it over tremendous distances, and this would suggest the expansiveness of Nebuchadnezzar's kingdom as he went North, South, East and West, conquering practically the whole known world. "Then I beheld till the wings thereof were plucked, and it was lifted up from the earth, and made

102 DANIEL

to stand upon the feet as a man".

In the first part of his history Nebuchadnezzar was a warrior, seeking by military might to build a huge empire, but in the later days of his rule he became a civilised man, ceasing his conquests, the wings were plucked off. "And he was lifted up from the earth". In the latter part of his reign, after his humiliation by God, when he grovelled on the earth like a beast, God transformed him. He was lifted up from degradation and depravity which marked him at the beginning of the book, "and a man's heart was given to him". This takes us back to the events of chapter four when he was converted and gave God glory, and in repentance sought to live for God. The lion is transformed; God changes lions. Nebuchadnezzar had an experience of God which is never recorded of any of the other emperors, and he stands out above them all as the head of gold.

"And I beheld another beast, a second like to a bear, and it raised up itself on one side, and it had three ribs in the mouth of it between the teeth of it; and they said thus unto it, arise, devour much flesh". Here is the second world empire, the Medo-Persian, the empire that was led by Darius the Mede and later by Cyrus the Persian, it is likened unto a bear. A bear crushes, and here is set forth the crushing power of the Medo-Persian empire, as they came, North and South, East and West crushing their enemies. Daniel says "I saw this bear leaning on to one side". Now the Medo-Persian empire was an alliance, a federation of Media and Persia, but in the course of time the Persian element predominated, found in the bear leaning to one side. Then we notice that it had three ribs in its mouth, probably referring to the three great cities of the empire. Nineveh, Babylon and Shushan the three great buttresses of the strength of the empire. The Medo-Persian empire was even more extensive than the Babylonian empire going down as far as India, so we get a sense of the command of God, "Arise, devour much flesh". But it is grand that all these kingdoms only arise when God

CHAPTER 7　　103

says so. All these kingdoms of the world are subject to God, although led by Satan, although dominated by the Devil, God has never relinquished His authority. People today are looking away to Russia, but we do not need to worry about Russia; Russia cannot move a hand or a foot until God says so, and if God says so, then of course, His will is best, but if God does not then they cannot move (In passing and it is interesting to remember that Russia has no very conspicuous part in the prophecy of God: she does play a part but not a very conspicuous part).

Verse 6, "After this I beheld, and lo another, like a leopard, which had upon the back of it four wings of a fowl; the beast had also four heads; and dominion was given to it". Here we come to the third empire, the Grecian empire, of Philip of Macedon and Alexander the Great. The Medo-Persian empire was overthrown by the Grecian empire and is likened unto a leopard, a very beautiful animal but it is spotted and, though the Grecian empire had some very beautiful features, alas, it was spotted by many dark stains and sins. Alexander the Great set up a centre of culture at Alexandria: it was one of his successors who ordered that the Hebrew Old Testament should be translated into Greek, now known as the Septuagint Version (LXX). Alexander the Great is stated to have said to Diogenes, the great Grecian moral philosopher, that if he had not been Alexander he would loved to have been Diogenes; so it would seem that he felt a sense of the limitation of his own grandeur and power. Yes, there were some beautiful things about Alexander's kingdom but, alas, it was spotted like a leopard and it was as cruel as a leopard, and we find Alexander spreading West and East and North and South in cruelty and hatred and indifference to others. You may know the story of how he is said to have sat down and cried because he had no more worlds to conquer: there is all the savagery that marks the leopard, and we read concerning Alexander, concerning the Grecian kingdom, that it "had upon the back of it four wings

DANIEL

of a fowl". (By the way, notice this recurrence of the number four). We read about the four winds and the four kingdoms, and here we have Alexander's kingdom with four wings of a fowl. Four is the universal number, North, South, East and West. When Peter sees the sheet in Acts chapter ten, carried up into heaven, it is knit at the four corners, the universal number. The four wings of a fowl would tell of the universality of Alexander's kingdom. Then we read, "it had four heads" speaking of Alexander's four generals, for his kingdom was shared jointly by Alexander and his four great generals.

We shall not say much about that just now because that will come out as we look at chapter eight. "And dominion was given to it" notice that, Who gives the dominion to it? God! You know God says "by me kings rule". In Romans chapter 13 we read "the powers that be are ordained of God" and no king has ever ruled except God gave him the kingdom. Now you may wonder how this can be explained, think of ruthless men like Hitler and Mussolini, did God give them their kingdoms? Yes, God gave them their kingdoms and they could not have ruled if God had not given them their kingdoms. In the book of Exodus God said to Pharoah "For this purpose I have raised thee up that I might show My glory in thee". Now do not let us stagger at these things: I cannot understand them any more than you. I do know that all the kings of the earth that have ever been have been raised up by God and even the Russian leader today with all his blasphemies and wickedness, God has raised up and that is why we must acknowledge the kings and rulers of the earth. You say, "How do you explain that?" Dear friends, I do not seek to explain it I simply fall back on the words of the Epistle to the Romans, "Can the thing say to the thing that formed it, why hast thou made me thus". I cannot understand it. I cannot understand why God ever raised up a man like the present Russian leader but it is true; God raises up the kingdoms of the earth. Of course, let me qualify this

CHAPTER 7

by saying that God never put it into their hearts to commit evil; it sprang from their own hearts, energised by Satan. But God raised up those men, knowing full well the things they would do. Now is God righteous? It would be blasphemy to suggest anything else, and we bow to the righteousness of God. "Shall not the judge of all the earth do right", and we trust, where we cannot see, and say in all things God is righteous.

Then Daniel says (verse 7) "After this I saw in the night visions, and behold a fourth beast, dreadful and terrible, and strong exceedingly; and it had great iron teeth; it devoured and brake in pieces, and stamped the residue with the feet of it, and it was diverse from all the beasts that were before it; and it had ten horns". Now, here is the Roman kingdom, and notice that it is specially marked by cruelty. The history of Rome teems with the records of cruelty. If you have ever read 'Gibbons Decline and Fall of the Roman Empire' you will know of the fearful cruelty of that nation: if you read, when you were a child going to school, the poems of Lord Byron, you will recall that he speaks of the terrible atrocities of Rome. In his tale of the dying gladiator butchered to make a Roman holiday he writes: "Shall he expire, and unavenged, arise ye Goths and glut your iron", protesting against the monstrous cruelty of Rome. You will remember how in Rome they had the stately Colosseum where the gladiators fought until one man was murdered just to satisfy the hearts of the people. Then, too, that in the reign of Nero and such men Christians were thrown to the lions. This is the fourth kingdom, strong as iron, telling of the strength of Rome: we see it, naked here before God in all its hideous cruelty; the wicked savagery and sadism of that monstrous empire. "And it was diverse from all the other beasts before it; and it had ten horns". Now, we shall see as we go on that this great kingdom of Rome is a ten kingdomed empire.

You notice what we saw in chapter 2; it starts with the Rome of the past and goes on to the Rome of the future. It

106 DANIEL

speaks of Rome here following after the Grecian empire; that is historically true. The Grecian empire was vanquished by the Roman empire but we find here that having spoken of Rome as following Greece it goes right on to the end and speaks of the time when the Roman Empire shall have ten kingdoms, referring to the future; so it jumps from the Rome of the past to the Rome of the future. Now that is the same phenomenon that we find in chapter 2; God stepping right over this present age, as we saw in the explanation of it. God is speaking of the earth here, nations on the earth; but today, in this present age He is not dealing with the earth; He is gathering out of the world a heavenly people, so God passes over this age altogether, passing it by as though it did not exist. It is an interval, a gap in the purposes of God, so God takes us up to the time of Christ crucified, Rome of the past and He passes right over this age and then goes on to the Rome of the time of tribulation. Beloved, that is a feature in all prophecy, as we found in chapter 2 so it is in chapter 7, and we will find it again in chapter 8 and again in chapters 9 and 11. It is a feature of all prophecy, and we find it right throughout the Old Testament.

Now, beloved, dare I say it, kindly and lovingly, that if those dear brethren who try to frighten us and sadden us, by suggesting that the Church will go through the tribulation, could only lay hold of that simple fact that we are living in an interval in the purpose of God, they would know that we never can go through the tribulation. Once God has finished with this age, then He will start to work on earth again and He will start exactly where He left off: He left off with Christ crucified and He will start back there, and the tribulation will follow on immediately from the rejection of Christ on the cross. If only the simplicity of this would grip God's dear people, how many a pitfall, how many an error, we would be saved from, such as that awful theory that the Church will go through the tribulation. We do thank God for the light of His precious Word that we are not looking for the

CHAPTER 7

107

tribulation, we are not looking for that horrible seven years, but for the very moment when the call shall come and our going to see Him and to be like Him for evermore. I tell you friends, if we had to go through the tribulation, the Lord's coming would be no blessed hope for me and it would be no blessed hope for any one of us, but because we know that He can come at anytime. Paul says to Titus "Looking for that blessed hope (the happy hope) of the glorious appearing of the great God and our Saviour Jesus Christ". Oh, beloved, with all respect to these dear brethren, without wishing to say anything unkind about them, do not let anybody rob you of your blessed hope in Christ, but, let us live in the light and power of it.

So then Daniel's prophecy steps right over from the Rome of the past to the time when the Roman Empire shall have ten kingdoms which acknowledge the authority of the Beast. "And I considered the horns and behold, there came up from among them another little horn, before whom there were three of the first horns plucked up by the roots: and behold, in this horn were eyes like the eyes of a man, and a mouth speaking great things". Well, that brings us to the Man of Sin of those days. The ten-kingdomed Roman empire will be formed and out of those ten kings will rise another king, (the little horn out of the Roman empire), who will be the Monarch of Rome; the ten kings will yield their power unto him and they will acknowledge this man. Three of the kings will resist him and they will be broken without hands, and this man, this Man of Sin, this Beast, this head of the revived Roman empire will dominate and lead the ten kingdom federation in opposition to God. There are many details about this into which we cannot enter now but, if you look in Revelation chapter 13 and Revelation chapter 17 you will find the counterpart of this; that Man of Sin that shall arise. You will read there about his ten kingdom empire and about his opposition to God and his union with the corrupt, the false church; exactly the same period that we are going to

108   DANIEL

consider now. Daniel gives the outline of it and Revelation chapters 13 and 17 give the details of it.

Daniel goes on in verse 9, after talking about kingdoms to speak about a kingdom. "I beheld till the thrones were cast down, and the Ancient of days did sit". When all these kingdoms have passed away the Lord is going to reign: when Babylon, Medo-Persia, Greece, Rome, Rome in its final character have all passed away, what is going to happen? The God of the Heavens will set up a kingdom. That takes us back to chapter 2, where Daniel said that "the God of the heavens shall set up a kingdom". This explains the truth of the Gospel of Matthew. Matthew speaks about the Kingdom of Heaven, referring to that day when the God of the heavens shall set up a kingdom and heaven will rule on earth, the fulfilment of the prayer that the Lord taught the disciples will come in, "Thy kingdom come", God's kingdom will come, and earth will be ruled by heaven; that is what God calls the Kingdom of the Heavens. "I beheld till the thrones were cast down, and the Ancient of days did sit".

The Ancient of days, of course, is God Himself, but why is He called the Ancient of days? It is because Babylon, Medo-Persia, Greece, and Rome pass; their kingdoms are marked by time; but here is the Ancient of days, God Himself; His kingdom is without beginning or end, "Whose garment was white as snow" telling of His absolute purity. By the way, it is interesting that in the Scriptures the expression 'white as snow' is used in four ways. In Mark 9 we read of the mount of transfiguration that His raiment was white as snow. Then in Psalm 68, when the Lord ascends and triumphs over His enemies, it says "it was white as snow in Salmon" telling how Salmon, the black forest, was bleached white with the bones of men under the government of the Lord. It is used in connection with the Lord's grace in Isaiah chapter 1 "Though your sins be as scarlet they shall be as white as snow"; God cleanses men in His grace. It is used concerning the restoration of backsliders in Psalm 51 "Purge me with

CHAPTER 7   109

hyssop and I shall be clean, wash me and I shall be whiter than snow". Mark 9 is concerning the Lord's glory, Psalm 68 His government, Isaiah 1 His grace, Psalm 51 His restoring power.

Well, here is the purity of God: it says, "His garment was white as snow and the head of his hair like the pure wool". Now white hair speaks of dignity, God says "Thou shalt rise up before the hoary head and honour the face of the old man"; white hair speaks of dignity, here it is God's dignity, God's Majesty. "His throne was like the fiery flame". Hebrews chapter 12 says, "Our God is a consuming fire", telling of His holinesss. "And His wheels as burning fire", telling of the intricacy of God's government. We sometimes talk about "wheels within wheels", deeply laid schemes, well the wheels of God here tell of His deeply laid plan. "A fiery stream issued and came forth from before Him"; telling of His judgment of His enemies. "Thousand thousands ministered unto Him, and ten thousand times ten thousand stood before Him"! There is the scene in Heaven; God in all His glory in that heavenly scene, corresponding to Revelation chaper 5, when ten thousand times ten thousand and thousands of thousands praised the glory of the living God. And then, "the judgment was set, and the books were opened"; that corresponds to Revelation chapter 5 also where we read "the book was opened". The book is the title deeds of the universe; God is about to claim the world as His own; He is about to put down Babylon, Medo-Persia, Greece and Rome; to overthrow these kingdoms and establish His own kingdom in righteousness, so the books are opened, the title deeds of the universe. In Revelation chapter 5 it is one book; here are books in the plural, because it brings in not only the taking of the title deeds of the universe but, the exercising of Divine judgment.

"I beheld then because of the voice of the great words which the horn spake: I beheld even till the beast was slain, and his body destroyed, and given to the burning flame".

DANIEL

Now that brings us to Revelation chapter 19. In Revelation chapter 19 this Beast, the head of the revived Roman Empire is making a savage attack on Jerusalem: he is seeking to destroy the people of God, and just in time, the Lord comes out from Heaven. It is the Lord's return to the earth, His coming in glory, and He comes back with His saints, who have been caught up seven years or more before and now He comes back with His saints and the beast is taken and cast into the lake of fire. It is the Lord appearing in government on behalf of, and for the deliverance of His people. Then we read, "As concerning the rest of the beasts, they had their dominion taken away: yet their lives were prolonged for a season and time". Now we saw previously that all these nations are going to be revived, Babylon, Medo-Persia, Greece and Rome. The monarch of Rome will be dealt with summarily: the Lord will destroy him (says the scripture) with the brightness of His coming, with the breath of His nostrils, and the Lord will cast him into the Lake of Fire when He comes with His saints; but the other kings will be spared a little while longer until the Lord sets up the judgment of the living nations, Matthew 25, when He gathers the nations together and separates the sheep from the goats. Then the Lord will judge those other kings, Babylon, Medo-Persia and Greece, but the judgment of the Roman monarch will be a summary judgment when the Lord appears in His Kingdom.

Now, from verse 9 to verse 12 we have the kingdom of the Ancient of days, God's kingdom, but in verses 13 and 14 we have the kingdom of the Son of Man. "I saw in the night visions, and, behold, one like the Son of Man came with the clouds of heaven, and came to the Ancient of days, and they brought Him near before Him. And there was given Him dominion, and glory, and a kingdom", here is the kingdom of the Son of Man. Oh, Beloved, God says in Psalm 2 "Why do the heathen rage", He says, "yet have I set my King upon my holy hill of Zion. He that sitteth in the heavens shall

CHAPTER 7

laugh, He shall have them in derision". The nations of the world are in rebellion against God; they have no room for God and His Christ, but God says "I have my King who is going to reign and nothing can stop it". The King is the Lord Jesus Christ, and then addressing His Son God says "ask of me and I will give thee the heathen for thine inheritance", and in the day which we are considering the Lord Jesus will ask of the Father and He will give Him the heathen for His inheritance and He will reign from shore to shore. Now notice it is the Kingdom of the Son of Man! Why Son of Man? The first time we read of the Son of Man in the New Testament is in Matthew chapter 8, "The Son of Man hath not where to lay His head": the last time we read of Him in the New Testament is in Revelation 14 when He comes to claim His own. Beloved, the Son of Man, whom the world cast out and would not give Him a place to lay His head, is coming in glory, to reign. We find Him in the dominion of His kingdom and He reigns in conjunction with the Father, and "His kingdom is an everlasting kingdom and His dominion, an everlasting dominion which shall not be destroyed". Oh beloved, the Lord is going to reign and He is going to reign forever and forever.

Now just a remark or two upon the interpretation of the vision in the latter part of the chapter, verses 15 to the end. You'll remember that we said there were additional details given in the interpretation, note verse 17. "These great beasts, which are four, are four kings, which shall arise out of the earth". In the vision we saw that they were arising out of the sea but in the interpretation we see that they were arising out of the earth, why is that? In the vision they come out of the sea, figuratively out of the trouble and the distress of nations, but in the interpretation they arise out of the earth in order to distinguish them from the Lord from heaven. Daniel has been telling us of the reign of Christ, the Lord from Heaven, Heaven's kingdom upon earth, so to

DANIEL

distinguish these beasts he says that they are of the earth whilst the Son of Man Who is going to reign is the Lord from (out of) Heaven; thus it is the earthly as distinct from the heavenly.

Then, verse 18, "But the saints of the Most High shall take the kingdom, and possess the kingdom for ever". Now in the vision we saw that the Son of Man will reign; in the interpretation it says that His people are going to reign. Beloved, in that day the Lord Jesus will reign and the remnant of Israel (that we spoke about earlier, delivered from out of the nations), and the remnant from the Gentiles will share in the glory of His government on earth. Further down the chapter it speaks of them as being "under heaven"; it is not speaking of the Church in glory, for that is heavenly; it is speaking of the earth here, (those under heaven) and the godly remnant out of Israel and those that were saved out of the Gentiles who will share with the Lord in the government of His kingdom on earth while you and I, of course, will be reigning with Him in Heaven.

Then, we read also, about the time of the reign of the beast. If we look at verse 25 "and they shall be given into his hand until a time and times and the dividing of time". If we look in the Revelation we read about 42 months which is three and a half years; and of 1260 days which is three and a half years according to the Hebrew reckoning: in the Hebrew year there were 360 days; and then we read of a time and times and half a time. A time means a year; times, two years; and half a time, half a year, making three and a half years. So now, we are directed to that same period of which the Revelation speaks. In the book of the Revelation we read of this Beast reigning for seven years divided into two sections of three and a half years. In the first three and a half years the Beast will favour the Jews; in the second three and a half years he will turn against the Jews. Here God is speaking of that second three and a half years and they will be delivered into the hand of the Beast for that time.

CHAPTER 7   113

Let me explain a little further. When the Lord comes He will take the Church home, then, probably not immediately but a little while after, this seven years will come in. The head of the revived Roman empire will make a covenant with the Jew and for three and a half years he will keep it: but after that time he will break it and then will come Israel's great trouble, what the Bible calls "the Great Tribulation", the latter part of the three and a half years. The whole 7 years are years of tribulation but the latter three and a half years after the Beast breaks his covenant are the years of greater tribulation when he will set up his image in Jerusalem and compel the Jews to worship him. He will blaspheme and profane the temple, then he will institute pollutions throughout Israel. Then, we read, concerning this Beast (verse 25), "and he shall wear out the saints of the Most High": now we did not read that in the vision, it does not say there that he would persecute the saints of the Most High (that is the remnant of Israel and the Gentiles), but we read of it here, "and think to change times and laws". Now in the Tribulation (when the Church has gone) they will keep the law of the Old Testament and they will keep the times of the Old Testament; times of the passover and unleavened bread and firstfruits and trumpets and atonement and tabernacles, but this Man of Sin will rise up and he will seek to do away with these times, he will seek to change the Jewish religion as it was laid down in the Old Testament, and so God will come in, in sovereignty. Then, verse 26, "But the judgment shall sit, and they shall take away his dominion, and the greatness of the kingdom under the whole heaven, shall be given to the people of the saints of the Most High, whose kingdom is an everlasting kingdom and all dominions shall serve and obey Him". Beloved, after the Beast and his forces are overthrown, Christ will reign, and His saints will reign with Him, and He will reign with a glory that shall never pass away.

114 DANIEL

"To Him shall endless prayers be made
And endless praises crown His head,
His name like sweet perfume shall rise
With every morning sacrifice".

And from every part of the world they will come with their tributes to Him and the world shall be filled with the glory of His Name.

"Peoples and realms of every tongue
Dwell on His love with sweetest song,
And infant voices shall proclaim
Their early blessings on His Name".

Oh beloved, as we look on that day, as we think of that glory, we can only say in our hearts, "Amen, even so come, Lord Jesus!".

Daniel Chapter 8

Mr. Bell read Daniel chapter 8

In reading this book the wonderful divine order of Holy Scripture is seen. In chapter 7 we entered into the purely prophetic part of the book and the four great kingdoms, Babylon, Medo-Persia, Greece and Rome were brought before us. Already we have been instructed regarding Babylon in chapters 1 to 5, and in chapter 8 we read of Medo-Persia and Greece. Chapter 9 deals with the Roman Empire, and all four are brought together in a comprehensive picture in chapter 11.

Chapter 8 can be divided into two parts; verses 1 to 14 show the immediate application of the vision; and all has been fulfilled historically, whilst verses 15 to 27 show the ultimate application of the vision; what is yet to be fulfilled. If God has fulfilled the first part we can rest assured that He will fulfil the second part.

At the beginning of the chapter we see that Daniel is no longer said to be at Babylon, but is transported in spirit to Shushan, the centre of the Medo-Persian Empire in the province of Elam, by the river Ulai, that he might be shown the kingdoms that would succeed Babylon. Elam means 'hidden times' and God is going to unveil these 'hidden times' to Daniel. Ulai means 'muddy waters' and God will reveal the sinfulness and depravity of the human heart as seen in these kingdoms.

Daniel's vision commences in verse 3 "and there stood before the river a ram which had two horns, and the two horns were high, but one was higher than the other, and the higher came up last". A ram speaks of strength and determination, and, as we read in verse 20, it represents the

115

116 DANIEL

kings of Media and Persia. One horn was higher than the other, reminding us of the bear in chapter 7 which leaned on one side; that is one side predominated. There were two elements in the kingdom ruled by Darius the Mede and Cyrus the Persian, but as time went on the Persian element became supreme. Verse 4, "I saw the ram pushing westward, northward and southward, so that no beast might stand before him"; this gives us an historic picture of the all-conquering Medo-Persian Empire, and we read "that there was no deliverance out of its hand". But God in righteousness comes in and deals with this ruthless kingdom, and in verse 7 the he-goat cast the ram down and there was no deliverance for it. The rough goat as indicated in verse 21 is the king of Greece "a goat out of the West". The he-goat, a rough, male goat speaking of its great authority and the fact that it was a mountain goat and 'touched not the ground' (verse 5) reminds us of the amazing rapidity with which this kingdom under Alexander the Great, the ruler of the Grecian kingdom, conquered the whole of the known world in twelve years. The goat's 'notable horn' (verse 5) speaks of this mighty monarch, who laid Medo-Persia low as is foretold in verse 6 "and he came to the ram that had two horns . . . and ran unto him in the fury of his power . . . and smote the ram and brake his two horns, and there was no power in the ram to stand before him, but he cast him down to the ground and stamped upon him".

When Alexander died (of the ravages of disease at the hand of God) or, as the scripture says, "the great horn was broken", at the height of his conquests, four other notable horns arose, and we know from history that Alexander's four generals divided the kingdom. Alexander's conquest of Medo-Persia was in the year 334 B.C. hence the prophecy was two hundred years before these events took place; a testimony to Divine revelation, the truth of God. Now verse 9 tells us that out of these four horns "a little horn came forth, becoming exceeding great, toward the South and

CHAPTER 8   117

toward the East, and toward the pleasant land", that is, Palestine. About 200 B.C. a great ruler, the Syrian, Antiochus Epiphanes arose who became the inveterate persecutor of the Jews. The spiritual leaders of Israel, the "host of heaven" (verse 10) were cast down and stamped upon; "the stars" (verse 10) the messengers of God, (see Revelation 2 and 3) those who sought to teach the people the law of God, shared their fate, and verse 11 "He magnified himself even to the prince of the host", and the daily sacrifice was banned, and God's sanctuary defiled and cast down.

At this time Israel was led by a great priest called Judas Maccabees, the leader of the priestly house of Israel entitled here "the prince of the host". These events took place between the end of the Old Testament and the beginning of the New Testament. During this time the books of the Apocrypha were written, not inspired of God or quoted by the Lord, but nevertheless historically true in greater part. Because of the people's transgression God allowed Antiochus Epiphanes to persecute them and take away the daily sacrifice, but in verse 13 we read of a "certain saint" who asked how long this was to be allowed. ('Saint' means 'holy one' and refers to an angel of God, but, a 'certain saint' could read 'a master of numbers' drawing attention to the importance of numbers in Scripture). He prophesies that the sanctuary should be cleansed in 2300 days, approximately 6 years, well, Antiochus Epiphanes attacked the sanctuary in the year 171 B.C. and in 165 B.C. the deprivation and corruption of this man ceased and the sanctuary was cleansed (verse 14). This iniquitous man attacked the priests and the Levites and would have burned the scriptures (verse 12). Here, Israel, under Judas Maccabees, arose as a man, and cast this inhuman monster out, to die (two years later) a miserable death. Men may deny the Word of God but it stands infallible and inviolate, and what it says will surely come to pass, exactly as God says.

This brings us to the second part of the chapter; the

118   DANIEL

revelation and the ultimate application of the vision. Verses 15 and 16 bring before us Gabriel, who is sent from heaven to make **Daniel understand** ; Gabriel is called the 'strong and mighty one' indicating that God has the power to carry out all He has said. In this present dispensation it is not the angels that enlighten us, but we who **enlighten them** Ephesians chapter 3 verse 10. So we see first that the interpretation emanates from heaven, then in verse 17 of its effect upon Daniel, "So he came near where I stood, and when he came I was afraid and fell upon my face, and he said unto me understand O son of man, for at the time of the end shall be the vision". Daniel was **made afraid**, he was filled with reverential awe and fell upon his face. Does the revelation of God in His Son have this effect on us today, or is there a lack of reverential fear of God in our gatherings. We would know greater power, if we approached the meetings with reverence, attended reverently to God's word, listening to His still small voice, continuing to meditate prayerfully on the message. Daniel was filled with reverential fear; **he was brought low.** God wants His word to humble us. Paul had a wonderful revelation in 2 Corinthians 12 but feared "lest he be exalted above measure" for the effect of God's revelation should be to bring us low, to recognize our worthlessness and vileness, yet to rejoice in God's wonderful grace in spite of all. Of course, all the vision we need today is in the Scriptures, none today has a special revelation.

So, firstly, Daniel was made afraid; secondly, he was brought low, and thirdly, he was made **unconscious of all around,** "in a deep sleep" (verse 18). Occupation with Christ will make us oblivious to all that goes on in this world. When the light shone upon Saul of Tarsus on the Damascus road he was blinded to all around, and God wants each of us to have this spiritual oblivion and complete occupation and communion with Christ. Fourthly, Daniel was **made to stand** "But he touched me and set me upright". The

CHAPTER 8   119

revelation of God in Christ can make us stand boldly before Him, and give us strength to be witnesses to Christ down here.

Now we have seen the emanation of the revelation from heaven and the effect of this upon Daniel, but now let us look at the enlightenment of the revelation concerning the people of God. Daniel was **made wise** in the things of God. Verse 19 "Behold I will make thee to know what shall be in the last time of the indignation, for at the time appointed the end shall be". If, like Timothy, we give ourselves wholly to these things, we too will be reverentially afraid, then humbled, occupied only with Christ, made to stand before God and men, and made wise with the wisdom that is first pure, then peaceable.

So God moves on from the past to the future and speaks of what "the end will be"; the end of time. Antiochus Epiphanes, although prominent in the past, was but a type of a greater monarch who was to come, "a king of fierce countenance and understanding dark sentences" (verse 23). He is called in Daniel 11 "the king of the north" and in Isaiah 10:5 "the rod of mine anger". In Daniel chapter 7 verse 8 we have the little horn that arose out of the Roman beast, the head of the revived Roman Empire, the man of sin, but here is the little horn that arises out of the Grecian beast, the head of the Assyrian Empire (when the church is no longer here Israel will have two notable enemies, to the West the Roman enemy, to the North the Assyrian enemy). This man is mighty but not by his own power for Satan is always behind the enemies of the people of God. In the tribulation "he will destroy many and through his policy and craft shall prosper". But, "he magnifies himself in his heart and sets himself up against the Prince of princes", Israel's true Messiah, the Lord Jesus Christ, God's King, and is "broken without hand (completely overcome). In Zechariah 14 at the battle of Armageddon, all God's enemies hurl themselves against Jerusalem (the man of sin from Rome, the king of the

DANIEL

North from Assyria, and the King of the South from Egypt) but Christ shall come and destroy them out of hand and set up His kingdom there. Throughout history, all who have persecuted God's people have never prospered. Finally in verse 27 "Daniel fainted" because he could not understand the revelation, but John is told in the Revelation chapter 10 "seal not the book". Daniel had a sealed book but now we have an open book, yet Daniel, although he could not understand the revelation "rose up and did the king's business", so we who do understand, should be much more about the King's business, serving the Lord with all our might, until He come.

Daniel Chapter 9

Mr. Bell read Chapter 9

Now we come to the great chapter of Daniel, the renowned prophecy of **Daniel's Seventy Weeks.** Daniel Chapter nine is the CRUX OF ALL PROPHECY; if we have an understanding of the ninth chapter of Daniel, then we have a grasp of the foundation of all God's prophetic word. The whole realm of prophecy is based upon the truth of the seventy weeks in this chapter, the key to all the prophetic revelations in God's precious word.

The chapter is in two sections; verses 1-19 and verses 20-27. In the first section (verses 1-19) is DANIEL'S PRAYER and then in the second section (verses 20-27) GOD'S ANSWER. In verses 1-19 we have 490 years **backward,** in verses 20-27 we have 490 years **forward.** What I mean is this, in verses 1-19 Daniel is pouring out his heart to God concerning Israel's failure, and he speaks about the desolations of Jerusalem; now Jerusalem had been desolate and the people captive for seventy years. Why was that so? If you turn back to II Chronicles chapter 36 and verse 21 you will find the reason is this—in the book of Leviticus chapter 23, God told Israel to keep a yearly sabbath every seventh year wherein they would let the land alone, and not till it nor cultivate it, but just let it lie fallow for a whole year, every seventh year. Now they neglected that, and so God made provision that the land would indeed keep its sabbath. Seventy times they had neglected the sabbath, so God declared that the land would lie fallow for the appropriate seventy years, on the principle if Israel did not fulfil the command of God, God Himself would ensure that sabbath would be kept. So the land lay fallow—desolate—for

DANIEL

seventy years, keeping the sabbath as God had said. Well now, the sabbath year was every seventh year, and here the land keeps sabbath for seventy years; now seventy times seven years is 490 years, thus God brings before us here the 490 years of Israel's failure. For 490 years the nation had failed to fulfil the sabbath of the land, so God gives the land 490 years of desolation. This is the 490 years of Daniel's **backward** look, to which I referred. Then, in verse 20 he looks forward for the same period of time—He says "seventy weeks are determined unto my people"—now as we shall find, these are weeks of years; just as you and I speak of a week of seven DAYS, Daniel here speaks of a week of seven YEARS. You will readily follow seventy times seven years is 490 years—thus he directs us, first 490 years back then 490 years on.

Verses 1-19 we notice first of all the harmony of the prophetic word, see verses 1 and 2— "In the first year of his reign I Daniel understood by books the number of the years whereof the word of the Lord came to Jeremiah that He would accomplish seventy years in the desolations of Jerusalem". Here we have Daniel the prophet referring to Jeremiah the prophet, and both are seen to be in beautiful harmony because both are inspired by the same Spirit of God. In Jeremiah—chapter 29—Jermiah prophesies that the land would be desolate seventy years, and as Daniel saw it was getting near to the end of the seventy years, he realised that the completion of the desolation of Jerusalem was near at hand. So we see the perfect harmony of these two great servants of God. Daniel in reading Jeremiah's prophecy rests all his faith upon it—what a testimony to the word used in chapter 11—"the scripture of truth". Before leaving verses 1 and 2 I should point out that this was in the "first year of Darius the son of Ahasuerus"—now Darius means "the restrainer" and how this chapter tells of God's restraint, as it reveals how for hundreds and hundreds of years God has been holding back until the appointed time, restraining the

CHAPTER 9

123

evil in the world until the time when He fulfilled His will. Darius you will note is the son of Ahasuerus, and Ahasuerus means "Lion King", and God is bringing before us that time when the Lord Jesus as the Lion of Judah shall take His dominion and rule and be glorified.

Verse 3 "and I set my face unto the Lord and prayed with fasting . . . ". Here from verse 3 to verse 6 we notice two things, sin and revival. Daniel prays to God and says we have sinned—he identifies himself with Israel's sin. Now you and I would not think Daniel had need to do that, for he was a holy man; we read at the end of the chapter that he was a man greatly beloved, three times we read of this expression in respect of Daniel—greatly beloved. Yet he says WE have sinned, identifying himself with the sin of the nation. Beloved, may I speak a word of advice for us all; whenever we speak of the failure of God's people, whenever we talk of departure, decay, backsliding, declension, deterioration—whenever we think of these things among the people of God, never let us say THEY have failed, THEY have done this, THEY are in a poor state, always let us associate ourselves with it—it is WE that are in this condition; always let us associate ourselves with our brethren. If this were true of Daniel's day it is more so now, for we are what Daniel never was; we are one body in the Lord and members one of another.

But in verses three to six we also find revival, and see that it was preceded by heart confession, by a pouring out of the heart to God. You know there are lots of movements for revival among God's people today accompanied by a great deal of excitement and emotion. Thank God for everything which goes on for Himself, but I often think how much better it would be if instead of all the excitement and display, there was first a pouring out of our hearts in confession to God. If there is unjudged sin among us, if there is tolerated evil, if there is condoned iniquity, if there is an allowing of things that are wrong, there will be a lack of blessing in our

124 DANIEL

efforts for God. When we are going to have some special movement for God, some special effort, a week or a fortnight of meetings, what a difference it would make if first of all there was Daniel's experience in verses 3-6, not so much hilarity, excitement, emotion, but a pouring out of our hearts in confessing, and a seeking to get right with God, and if necessary to get right also one with another. Now notice in verses 7 and 8 Daniel says "Righteousness belongeth unto Thee"—here he acknowledges that righteousness belongs to God. Then in verses 9-14 he says "Mercies and forgiveness belong to God". Daniel's confidence in God for the great revival that was coming in Israel is based upon two things.

(1)   That to God belongs righteousness (verses 7 & 8)
(2)   To God belongs mercies (verses 9-14).

Daniel looks and he says, Lord; during all these years, during all the years of Israel's history, Thou hast been righteous, Thou hast fulfilled Thy word Lord, doing all that was promised, accomplishing all Thou saidst Thou wouldst do, never failing amidst our unfaithfulness—or to use words which were spoken later "If we believe not yet Thou abidest faithful"—so Daniel extols the righteousness of God. Then in verses 9-14 he says (in effect) "Here, we are, we have slain Thy prophets Lord, departed from Thy word, polluted Thy temple, we have defiled Thy land, we have failed in our obligations to Thee, but Lord, to Thee belong mercies and forgivenesses, even though we have rebelled against Thee". May I commend this attitude to you and me; I wish, oh how I wish, there was more of this in evidence among God's people. When faced with the need of deeper spirituality, more fruitful service; more energetic endeavours for Himself, oh if there was a looking within; a searching of our hearts, a confession of sin, a seeking to get right one with another, what a difference it would make. Mr. J. N. Darby used to say that the point of departure is the point of

CHAPTER 9

recovery, and so it is in the Christian life. Where we went wrong, is where we get right. That, then, is the principle, beloved, in verses 7-14. Daniel looks up and says "Lord, Thou hast been righteous" and then "We have been utterly sinful and we seek the mercy of God to get right with Thee". That is the secret of triumph in the Christian life, and may I say that we are all very concerned today about the lack of blessing, the lack of fruit, but when our assemblies, when the Christians where we are, ourselves included, get to the point that we seek to remove the impediments, the hindrances, the stumblingblocks, that is when blessing will come, but it will never come any other way; remember that, fellow-believers, it will never come any other way.

In verses 15 and 16 Daniel prays like this "And now O Lord our God that has brought thy people forth out of the land of Egypt with a mighty hand and has gotten Thee renown etc."—in these verses he seeks for blessing on the ground of redemption "Lord," he says, "Thou hast redeemed us—brought us forth out of Egypt, and so we seek Thy blessing". Then in verses 17 to 19 he seeks for blessing on the ground of the holiness of God—see in verse 19 "for thine own sake O Lord, for thy people and thy city are called by thy name." So in verses 15 and 16 Daniel asks for blessing, forgiveness and restoration because Israel was redeemed of the Lord; he falls back on the basis of redemption—and you know, fellow believers, it is grand in all the circumstances of the Christian life to fall back on the shed blood of the Lord Jesus Christ—"Lord I have sinned, I know I have gone astray, I know I have done wrong, but the blood was shed for me and on the ground of that precious blood I seek to be restored to fellowship with Thee". Then in verses 17 to 19 he asks for the blessing on the basis of God's glory; he asks the Lord to bless for His own sake—"because the city is called by thy name". Child of God, never forget that God has put His name upon us, God's glory is bound up in us, and God is going to bless us richly and abundantly and wonderfully for

126   DANIEL

His own glory; for the glory of His name. Just think for a moment fellow believers, God has promised you wonderful blessing; if those promises of blessings were not fulfilled (and of course it would be blasphemous to countenance the very thought that they might not be kept—but just suppose for the sake of illustration that they were not kept) then the devil could point at the failure to fulfil the promises—God's glory is bound up in the fulfilment of His word and He is going to fulfil it all, for His own glory. So we see, God's glory is bound up in His people, that is the thought, and in that beloved Psalm 23 "He leadeth me in the paths of righteousness for His name's sake"—because His glory is bound up in His people.

We come now to the next half of the chapter—verses 20 to 27, and here we are occupied with the **Seventy Weeks**—the 490 years—**onward.** We have thought of the 490 years backward of Israel's failure, now let us look at the 490 years forward. Notice verse 20 "And whiles I was speaking and praying and confessing my sin, and the sin of my people Israel, and presenting my supplication before the Lord for the holy mountain of my God; yea whiles I was speaking in prayer, even the man Gabriel whom I had seen in a vision at the beginning, being caused to fly swiftly, touched me, about the time of the evening oblation". Well, now, in verses 20 and 21 we have the **beginning of revelation.** Daniel looks back to the previous revelation (see chapter 8) to Gabriel who brought it then, now here is Gabriel again. By the way, chapter 8 is connected to the beginning of prophetic events, chapter 9 with the end of prophetic events and it was Gabriel at the beginning (chapter 8) and Gabriel at the end (chapter 9)—thus we have the beginning of revelation. Now look at the next two verses, here we have **the beginning of supplication**—verse 22—"and He informed me, and talked with me and said, "O Daniel, I am now come forth to give thee skill and understanding, at the beginning of thy supplication the commandment came forth and I am come

CHAPTER 9

to show thee for thou art greatly beloved". Is it not grand just to think how Gabriel came at the beginning of supplication—fellow believers, God is far more ready to hear than we to ask—so here we find that the answer comes from God at the beginning of Daniel's supplication. Oh, child of God, do not let us think that God is reluctant to bless, do not let us doubt the goodness and providence of God, or have misgivings regarding His grace, His mercy; He is truly far more ready to answer than we to ask.

This brings us then to the prophecy of the **Seventy Weeks,** and I want you to look at it carefully with me, and this is what we will find:—first of all, in verse 24, we read about Seventy Weeks; in verse 25 we read of Seven Weeks, then in verse 25 again we have three score and two weeks (i.e. 62 weeks) in verse 27 we read about one week, and later in the same verse about half a week (i.e. "in the midst of the week"). So we read here about 70 weeks, 7 weeks, 62 weeks, 1 week and ½ of a week—what is all this about? First, let me say that the word "week" is **a period of seven;** seven days, seven weeks, seven years or seven hundreds of years, the word week simply means a period of seven, like the Latin heptad—a period of seven. Well now, in this case, **the Seventy Weeks are weeks of years, not weeks of days.** Seventy weeks as we know them now would be 70 times 7 days, but these weeks are weeks of **years** so it is 70 times 7 years. Let me illustrate what I mean. Away back in the book of Genesis (chapter 29) when Jacob was serving Laban, he served seven years for Leah, and then seven years for Rachel. Now Laban said about Rachel "Fulfil her week, and I will give her unto you"—so Jacob served a further seven years for Rachel, and Laban called that "a week",—Jacob worked a week of years for Rachel. These Seventy Weeks are weeks of years then. The verse says (verse 24) "Seventy weeks are determined upon thy people, and upon thy Holy City".

I want you to notice the wonderful goodness of God; Daniel is occupied with the seventy years of captivity in

DANIEL

Babylon, he realises the time is at an end, and he asks God to bless them, now God comes in and assures him He is going to bless and deliver the nation from Babylon, but in the goodness of God he takes him much further. Daniel is told that truly his people will have a deliverance now, they will veritably be taken back to Canaan their own beloved land, but more than the fact of the immediate fulfilling of God's promise, Daniel is to have his eyes opened and be pointed on hundreds of years ahead to the complete, the final, the ultimate deliverance of Israel. So God gives Daniel far more than he asked for; Daniel was thinking of a present deliverance, a present restoration to Canaan, but God opens his eyes to a final deliverance. Beloved, in Ephesians chapter 3 we read "Unto Him who is able to do exceeding abundantly, above all that we ask or think, unto Him be glory." Child of God, God is able to give us not merely what we ask in prayer, but heaped up, pressed down, shaken together and running over. So it is here, and I venture to suggest that in my experience it is always so, God always gives far more than we ask or think.

"Seventy weeks determined upon thy people and upon thy holy city." **Thy** people; well, who were Daniel's people? Israel, the nation of Israel. "**Thy** holy City"—what was Daniel's holy city? Jerusalem. Child of God I beg of you notice this—**the seventy weeks of prophetic revelation have to do with Israel and Jerusalem. (**"Thy people; and **Thy** Holy City"). You know, if we got hold of this we should never be troubled with the idea current today that the Church will pass through the Tribulation, if we realised this great fact we would appreciate that the Church cannot—cannot possibly pass through the Tribulation. Notice here, in the centre of prophecy, "Seventy weeks are determined upon **thy** people and **thy** holy city". In the book of the Revelation chapters 6-18 we get the Great Tribulation, and the Church is never once mentioned in it; men put the Church there but God never does. Oh, child of God, with all my heart, and

CHAPTER 9

increasingly as the days go on, I thank God that I can expect Him at any moment; there is nothing left to be fulfilled before the Church goes home to be with Christ.

So, "Seventy weeks are determined upon thy people and upon thy holy city". Now in those seventy weeks God is going to do seven things— (1) to finish the transgression (2) to make an end of sin (3) to make reconciliation for iniquity (4) to bring in everlasting righteousness (5) to seal up vision (6) and prophecy and (7) to anoint the most holy. Here then, in seventy weeks, that is 490 years, God says He is going to do seven things for Israel. God opens to Daniel a vista of prophecy. God tells him to look 490 years ahead (70 x 7) and promises to do seven things for Israel in that time. First God is going to finish the transgression, and bring in a time when Israel will no more transgress against God. God is also going to make an end of sins; there will come a time when Israel will no more sin against God. God will also make reconciliation for iniquity. Here then we get (1) transgression—the "going beyond", the act of sin (2) Sins, the nature, the essence of sin itself (3) Iniquity—evil in the thought. So we have evil in the act (transgression) in the essence (sin) and in the thought (iniquity)—and God says He will bring in a time when He will put all three away, and purge from Israel their sin, their transgression and their iniquity.

Then, from this, the negative side, God goes on in His revelation to Daniel with the positive side—"to bring in everlasting righteousness, to seal up vision and prophecy, and to anoint the most Holy". God promises to bring in to Israel everlasting righteousness. How will that be?—Let us go back in thought, like Daniel, to Jeremiah's prophecy, to "the Lord their righteousness" (Jehovah Tsidkenu) for it is by the Lord their righteousness that Israel is going to be brought one day into everlasting righteousness—I mean, of course, those of Israel who are alive at that time. "And to seal up the vision and prophecy"— beloved, God has lingered

130 DANIEL

long; we saw how this chapter began with Darius the restrainer, God has indeed lingered long, but there is coming a time (God says so) when He is going to seal up vision and prophecy. Vision is inward; prophecy is outward; and God declares here that one day He will accomplish the inward visions and the outward prophecies, and fulfil His word. Many years ago David Hulme the Scottish atheist, an infidel, used to blaspheme God saying He had never fulfilled His promises and prophecies to Israel. Well, Peter says "God is not slack concerning His promises", and God WILL, He will unquestionably, fulfil all His word by and by—II Corinthians chapter 1 says "In Christ is the yea and amen of all the promises of God". All the promises are "Yea" that is affirmation, and "Amen" that is confirmation; affirmed and confirmed in God's beloved Son. Then "to anoint the most Holy"—we have seen in our recent studies how after the Lord has taken His Church home, seven years or more afterwards He will come back **with** His Church; He will cleanse the temple and there will be a pure temple in Jerusalem, so here we see Him "anointing the most Holy", the most holy place of the temple God will cleanse by and by.

First, then, God tells us **what** He is going to do; He is going to do these seven things. Then He tells us for whom He is going to do them; Israel. God then goes on to tell us when He is going to do them, and how He will do them. "Know therefore, that from the going forth of the commandment to restore and rebuild Jerusalem unto the Messiah, the Prince, shall be seven weeks and three score and two weeks." God thus says that "from the going forth of the commandment" shall be seven weeks (that is 7 x 7 years = 49 years) and sixty two weeks (7 x 62 years = 434 years). Why does God single out these periods? Well, first, the 49 years (the seven weeks)—"the street shall be built again and the wall even in troublous times;" the 49 years (the seven weeks) then had to do with the rebuilding of Jerusalem. It took 49 years to

CHAPTER 9   131

rebuild Jerusalem. In Nehemiah chapter 2 we read how they came up out of Babylon, and Zerubbabel and Joshua led them in the rebuilding of the city and the rebuilding of the wall and this took 49 years. So we see the first seven weeks (the 49 years) are occupied with the rebuilding of the city.

Then Daniel records there will be a period of 62 weeks (434 years) which with the 7 weeks (49 years) makes 69 weeks. Now 69 weeks makes (7 x 69) 483 years. Thus God is revealing to Daniel that from the going forth of the **commandment** to build the city and the temple to the coming of Messiah, the Prince, is 483 years. Here God makes a definite prophecy, and the Bible stands. or falls by that prophecy. Let us face the matter quite clearly—if it is true then this (Mr. Bell held up his Bible) is God's inspired word—if God prophesied the very year when Christ would come, and this is true in the event, then the Bible is veritably inspired of God, **but** if it is not true, then the Bible is a lie. Now which is it? Is God's word right or is it wrong? Let us test it—four hundred and eighty three years. Now the **command** to which God refers is given in Nehemiah chapter 2, it is recorded there that Artaxerxes issued an **edict** that Jerusalem should be rebuilt; that was in the year 445 B.C. Here God arranges His plan, it will be 445 years from here to Christ. The Lord came, and He died in the year 32 A.D. you will see then that 445 years plus 32 years gives us 477 years, but then the Hebrew year was a year of 360 days, our year has 365 days.

We have just reckoned the period in accordance with our current reckoning by our (Julian) calendar, but this is a Jewish prophecy and must be calculated by the Hebrew calendar (of 360 days) and the difference is approximately six years (483 x 5 days). Now we had 445 years plus 32 years to give us 477 years and we add on 6 years for the variation between the Julian and Hebrew calendars and so we get 483 years; the time that the Book of Daniel says—69 weeks of years (483 years). Thus it was in very truth 483 years from the

132 DANIEL

going forth of the commandment, to Messiah, the Prince. Now let me say in qualification here that this is a very rough calculation, and because of calendar changes over the years is not exact. I am not a mathematician, and cannot demonstrate to you how we must make allowances for such things as the inter-calary month of the Jewish year which was based on the lunar cycle as against our solar calculation, but I wanted to demonstrate to you in a simple way which we can all readily follow, how the 483 years is arrived at. But we can turn to the scholarship of certain authorities in order to substantiate the accuracy of the prophecy.

If you consult the book by Sir Robert Anderson—"The Coming Prince"—you will see how Sir Robert in collaboration with the Astronomer Royal, and calculating upon the basis of the solar year, demonstrates that from the going forth of the commandment (Nehemiah 2) to the time of the Lord's entry into Jerusalem on an ass was 483 years **to the very day.** Notice what Daniel says "Messiah shall come and be cut off" and Sir Robert Anderson proves by calculations from the solar year that this was fulfilled to the very day. After 483 years Christ came, rode into Jerusalem on the back of an ass—and was "cut off". God's word fulfilled to the very year even to the very day. Other authorities have approached along different lines, but the amazing thing is this, whichever way they approach it, they all come to the same answer. For example, Mr. Thomas Newberry calculates upon the dates of Archbishop Ussher—as you will no doubt appreciate, the dates in the margin of our bible do not belong to the bible itself but were put in about 400 years ago by Archbishop Ussher—and Mr. Newberrry taking up these dates produces the same answer as the others that it was exactly 483 years from the commandment of Nehemiah 2 to the entry of the Lord into Jerusalem. William Hoste in his book on Daniel using the basis of the anomalistic year (which allows for the excess hours over the 365 days which is regulated by our leap year

CHAPTER 9   133

system) produces the same result. So you see, beloved, how God has ordered His word; you can calculate it how you will, you can approach it from what angle you choose, like Sir Robert Anderson from the solar year, like Thomas Newberry from Ussher's dates, like William Hoste from the anomalistic year—but you come to exactly the same point, that 483 years after the edict went forth, the Lord rode into Jerusalem on the back of an ass, and was "cut off". Here is **the most sensational prophecy,** I submit, of all divine revelation, that God recorded the very time when my Lord should die upon Calvary, and it is there in His word for all to see.

Well now, let us proceed—"After three score and two weeks shall Messiah be cut off, but not for Himself" (or literally "He shall be cut off and have nothing")—"and the people of the Prince that shall come shall destroy the city and the sanctuary". Forty years (approximately) after the Lord died, that is in the year 70 A.D. Titus, the Roman general marched in and Jerusalem was destroyed. "And the end thereof shall be with a flood, and unto the end of the war desolations are determined". Jerusalem is desolate till this very day. But then (in verse 27) we pass immediately from that which is to us now history, **into the future—**"and He shall confirm the covenant with many for one week". Now, beloved, that has not happened yet. Here is God saying that in seventy weeks (or 490 years) Israel shall be cleansed from all unrighteousness, but that has not happened yet, well how do you account for it: **Sixty-nine weeks have been fulfilled,** leaving only **one week to be fulfilled.** When? Beloved, you and I are living in an **interval** between Daniel's sixty-ninth and seventieth week. We are living in a gap, a parenthesis, a hiatus, between weeks 69 and 70. Well why is that? Notice what we said at the beginning—"seventy weeks are determined upon **thy** people and **thy** holy city", but there is no such thing as Daniel's people today, for they are scattered all over the world, and God is not dealing with Daniel's

134 DANIEL

people—He is dealing now with the Gentiles—see Acts 15 "God visited the Gentiles to take out of them a people for His name". Furthermore, there is no such thing as "Thy holy city" today, Jerusalem is in ruins and the Mohammedan Mosque of Omar stands on the site of the temple of Israel. The seventy weeks have been broken off, because of Israel's rejection of Christ, because of their crucifixion of God's Son. God has set Israel aside. If we turn to Micah chapter 5 we read how God says "they will smite the judge of Israel with a rod upon the cheek, therefore I will give them up". At Calvary Israel did indeed smite the Judge of Israel with a rod upon the cheek, so God has given them up, and the seventieth week has never been fulfilled. So in this present age God is not dealing with Israel, with Jerusalem, but with the Church, and He is not dealing with earth, but with heaven.

Now, fellow believers, do you not see what I mentioned before, God, cannot—I say it reverently—God cannot turn to Israel, until He has removed the Church. Today, Israel is broken off, and God is dealing with the Gentiles and God cannot again turn to Israel until He has concluded His work with the Gentiles. This age in which we now live is passed over and there will come a day, and it could be today, when God will have finished His dealings with the Gentiles, and the Church will be taken home, and THEN God will fulfil the seventieth week. **Then** He will turn again to Israel, and fulfil the 70th week—have you got it, fellow believers? We live between the 69th and 70th week of Daniel, a gap in the prophetic purposes of God, and God is now gathering out for Himself a heavenly people, and at any moment that time will be over and the Church will be "for ever with the Lord"—then again God will turn, and He will start exactly where He left off—He left off at week 69; He will start again at week 70.

So we jump right over to the end "and He shall confirm the covenant with many for one week". Now you notice we have

CHAPTER 9

before us the Roman Empire, we saw "the people of the Prince that shall come shall destroy the city and the sanctuary", that was the Roman Empire under their general Titus, so it is the Roman Empire that is in view, and it is the Prince of the Roman Empire that will "confirm the covenant"—the Man of Sin, the Beast, of whom we have been speaking earlier. He will make a covenant with the Jews (of that day) for seven years, and "in the midst of the week, he shall cause the sacrifice and the oblation to cease". Here we see the great Man of Sin in a coming day, making a seven year treaty with the Jews, and for half of the week, that is half of the seven year period ($3\frac{1}{2}$ years) everything will be alright between him and the Jews; but after three and a half years he will set up his image in the temple and he will do away with their sacrifices, and instead of seeking to worship God, they will have to worship him. This will start the second half of the week (of seven years) the three and a half years of Great Tribulation. You know the whole of the seven years are called the Tribulation, but the latter half particularly is the Great Tribulation. In the first half of the seven years the beast is friendly towards Israel, in the middle of the seven years he breaks his friendship, breaks his covenant, does away with the sacrifices and sets up his image to be worshipped by them, then the Great Tribulation, the more dreadful part of it, begins as Israel is desolated by its enemies. Then will come to pass what the Lord said in Matthew 24 "let them that are in Judea flee to the mountains" for then there will be bloodshed and slaughter and savagery as the beast persecutes the Israel of God, as he persecutes those who refuse to bow to his image, refuse to bear his mark, and refuse to worship him, that is the persecution of the Godly remnant of Israel.

Finally, "and for the overspreading of abominations he shall make it desolate". God speaks of idolatry as an abominable thing and because of this abomination, the idolatry, he will desolate the land—and then "even until the

136 DANIEL

consummation, and that determined shall be poured upon the desolate". That last word "desolate" means literally "the desolator". The Beast will desolate the land, he will defile the land, he will corrupt the land, "until the consummation"—the end, the conclusion—and then what—the indignation of God, "for the consummation, and that determined shall be poured upon the desolater". At the end of the seven years the Lord will appear, and He will appear **with** the Church—you and I will come back with Him—and as the Lord appears Israel, the true Israel, the remnant, is being persecuted by the beast; ravaged, destoyed, defiled, murdered, butchered, and then the Lord will come in and pour His indignation upon the desolater, upon the Beast—II Thessalonians chapter 2 says "The Lord shall destroy with the brightness of his coming". He will come in the judgment of God and save His people from the hand of His enemies.

Well, now we have in Daniel chapter 9, seventy weeks, seven weeks, sixty-two weeks, one week, half a week. The seventy weeks, the 490 years in which God's purposes with Israel will be accomplished; seven weeks, the 49 years, the time of the rebuilding of the city; sixty two weeks, the period of 434 years between the building of the city and the time when Christ rode into the city and was "cut off". So we have sixty-nine weeks altogether, 483 years, from the going forth of the edict to rebuild Jerusalem to the time when Christ was cut off. Now God has turned aside from Israel, and we are in an interval between the sixty-ninth and seventieth week, but, when God has taken out the Gentile bride His heavenly Church—home to be with the Lord—then the seventieth week will come in and the Head of the revived Roman Empire will make a covenant with the Jews for seven years. Half way through the seven years the Roman head will break the covenant, and set up his own image and persecute the Jews, until at the end of the seven years the Lord shall appear for the deliverance of His people.

CHAPTER 9

137

Beloved, you and I are the heavenly Church, we belong to a Man in the Glory, but never let us forget the nation of Israel, for they are God's earthly people and God loves them still and God's thoughts are with them—so He tells us "Pray for the peace of Jerusalem". Thus we rejoice in Jeremiah's words (Jeremiah 30) that it is the time of Jacob's trouble, but they are going to be saved. Israel will pass through that awful seven years and only a third part of them will come through, but God will refine them and purify them and bless them, and settle them in their own land. Never again shall they sin against God, never again rebel, and never again shall the assassins' hand be found amongst them, but the glory of the Lord will fill His people. Then they shall be, as God calls them prophetically, in a real and true sense—Israel My glory.

Daniel Chapters 10 to 12

Mr. Bell read chapters 10 and 12

We come now to the final portion of the prophecy of Daniel. Chapter 10 tells us of a conflict in the heavens. Chapter 11 tells us of a conflict between the nations. Chapter 12 tells us of a conflict among the people of God.

In chapter 10 there are four things for our consideration. In verses 1-3 we have Daniel seeking, in verses 4-9 Daniel seeing, in verses 10-17 Daniel speaking, in verses 18-21 Daniel strengthened.

Verses 1-3, "In the third year of Cyrus king of Persia a thing was revealed unto Daniel, whose name was Belteshazzar, and the thing was true, but the time appointed was long; and he understood the thing, and had understanding of the vision. In those days I Daniel was mourning three full weeks". Here Daniel, conscious that a great move was about to begin, conscious that God is going to take His people out of Babylon and bring them to Palestine, he seeks for illumination from God as to when all this is to come to pass. He continues fervently in prayer for the answer to come. Such was his diligence in prayer that for three weeks he ate no pleasant bread, he drank no wine and did not anoint himself but ceaselessly week after week, for three weeks he pleaded, supplicated, interceded and sought the guidance and enlightenment of God. Here is Daniel seeking. May I ask, child of God, are we characterized by that continuous, unremitting, unceasing search after the mind of God, searching after guidance and enlightenment, searching after instruction, searching after fellowship with God? Daniel was tireless in it, he did not relax, he did not cease until he had the mind of God. Forgive me saying this,

140   DANIEL

but there is an awful lot of light, superficial christianity today, we read the Word, perhaps we read a portion every day and thoughts come before us and when we lack understanding we put the Word down. Daniel did not do that, he went on earnestly seeking understanding and enlightenment of the Word of God. Beloved, God wants that same tenacity, that same steadfastness, that same devotion in you and me, earnestly, tirelessly seeking for light from God.

In verses 4-9 we have Daniel seeing. "And in the four and twentieth day of the first month, as I was by the side of the great river, which is Hiddekel (by the way it is so wonderful here; the river Hiddekel is the Tigris and the word means swift flowing. Daniel has been occupied with the long delay, he has been occupied with the fact that the time is long; now he is standing beside the river Hiddekel, the swift flowing river. Daniel, look at that river, swift in its flow, and yet it seems a long time for God to work out His purposes, there seems to be nothing moving but, in God's own appointed time, swift as the river Hiddekel, God's purposes will ripen, a nation will be born in a day, things shall be changed in a night; with the swiftness of the Hiddekel, God's purpose will be carried into effect, and so the river stands out as a lesson of the swiftness of the purposes of God. I should perhaps mention that the Hiddekel was one of the four rivers of Genesis chapter 2, flowing out of Eden. There was the Pison, the Gihon, the Hiddekel and the Euphrates. Beloved, here whilst we are dealing with the end of time God takes us back to the beginning of man's history, and that is characteristic right throughout the Bible. If we turn to Ezekiel chapter 38, in relation to the end of time, the time of the setting up of the Lord's kingdom, we find there, Gog, Magog, Tubal, Mesheck, Togarmah and Gomer, where do all these names come from? They come from Genesis 10. Here God, at the end of time, is bringing in what originated at the beginning. There is a definite purpose working all through the Word of

CHAPTERS 10 - 12 141

God, a definite thread of Divine purpose and foresight and from the beginning we see that line of Divine purpose working right through until the end. The books of the Bible are not haphazard, they are not strung together anyhow, there is a Divine purpose underlying all the things of God's precious Word, and so when we come to the end of time we see the names jumping into life that were given to us at the very beginning: so it is here with the river Hiddekel).

"Then I lifted up mine eyes, and looked, and behold a certain man clothed in linen, whose loins were girded with fine gold of Uphaz". This man clothed in linen is a picture of the Lord Jesus Christ. We see in Leviticus that linen is not warm to the flesh, it does not engender fleshly warmth; it speaks of the character of Christ in which there was no fleshly heat, no fleshly passion; He was pure and He was holy. "His loins were girded with gold", now when the Lord Jesus Christ was on earth (John 13) He girded Himself with a towel to wash His disciples feet: here He is in glory and He is girded with gold. The lowly Servant is going to be exalted by and by and the girdle of the towel will be superseded by the girdle of gold. "His body also was like the beryl", a very beautiful stone speaking of the Lord's beautiful humanity. "And His face as the appearance of lightning". Lightning in Matthew 24 is a figure of judgment "as the lightning shineth from one part of heaven to the other, so shall be the coming of the Son of Man, two shall be lying in bed, one taken and the other left", a picture of the Lord coming in judgment. "And his eyes as lamps of fire", telling of the discernment of the Lord. "He discerns the thoughts afar off". "And his arms and His feet like in colour to polished brass, and the voice of His words like the voice of a multitude". "Feet like unto polished brass; a symbol of the Lord's endurance, the enduring One, who endures throughout the ages, the Rock of Ages. "And His voice is the sound of a great multitude", you have heard a voice of a great multitude, how impressive it is, how startling it sounds. Here it is the voice of the Lord in

142 DANIEL

judgment; not the still small voice of grace, but the voice of the Lord in judgment.

"And I Daniel alone saw the vision". Beloved, if you and I are going to see visions of the Lord, visions in the Word itself, if you and I are going to behold the Lord, we will have to know what solitude is. Child of God, there must be times in the life when we even withdraw from God's people and in solitude discern the glory of the Lord. And then, the Lord speaks to him and He says "Now I am come to make thee understand what shall befall thy people in the last days". Notice too that there is an indication given to Daniel of what had happened when three weeks before as he prayed, this angel (who is a picture of the Lord) was sent to Daniel, but the prince of Persia came to resist him. Now at the beginning of the chapter we read that Cyrus was the king of Persia but obviously this does not now refer to Cyrus but to the satanic prince of Persia. Beloved, behind the rulers of this world there are satanic princes who govern the kingdoms on earth. So we get a picture here of conflict in the heavens, the satanic prince of Persia warring against the angel of God and Michael the archangel. Michael is mentioned here as "your prince"; in chapter 12 he is the angel that stands up for the people of God, for Israel, and Michael is the only person in scripture who is ever called the archangel and we only read of one archangel. So then there is conflict in the heavens, and then when the angel had spoken unto Daniel, he set his face toward the ground and he tells how the angel came and strengthened him and made him to stand up. There is much that could be said on chapter 10 but I must be content to mention just this; in the chapter there are three "touches"; verse 10, "and behold a hand touched me, which set me on my knees", and then Daniel stood up. First God touched him and made him stand, verse 10. Now look at verse 16 "and behold, one like the similitude of the sons of men touched my lips: then I opened my mouth". God touched him and made him speak. Verse 18 "Then there came again and touched me

CHAPTERS 10 - 12   143

one like the appearance of a man, and he strengthened me". So in verse 10 God touched him and made him stand, in verse 16 He touched him and made him speak, in verse 18 He touched him and made him strong. Beloved, Daniel faced with these wonders of prophecy felt overwhelmed, helpless, it brought him low, but in the light of all that prophetic truth God touched him and made him stand, speak and made him strong. We also feel overwhelmed, astounded, carried away by all this wealth of prophetic truth; we feel that there is no spirit left in us, but God can make us stand up and live out this truth, God can fit us to practise this truth, fit us to apply this truth. He can touch us and make us stand, touch us and make us speak as His witnesses, touch us and make us strong in the Lord and in the power of His might. There, reluctantly we shall have to leave chapter 10.

Now I want you to glance for a moment at chapter 11. We said that chapter 11 spoke of the Conflict of Nations and it divides itself like this: Verses 1 to 31 the conflict in the ages past. From verse 32 to the end of the chapter the conflict in the ages yet to come. In verse 1-31 we read of the conflict between Assyria, the king of the North, and Egypt, the king of the South. Then from verse 32 to the end of the chapter we find the king of the North and the king of the South banded together and attacking a common foe, the Roman Empire. Verses 1 to 31 speaks of the warfare that lasted for centuries between the king of the North and the king of the South, Assyria and Egypt. This covers centuries of history, from about 550 B.C. the time when Daniel wrote, to just before the time when the Lord came to earth, a period of about 550 years. Every detail of these verses has been historically fulfilled, men of the world have staggered at it. In the third century a heathen unbeliever and an enemy of Christianity rose up stating that this chapter, Daniel chapter 11, had been written after the event; it was so absolutely perfect. This is a wonderful tribute to the inspiration of God's precious Word.

DANIEL

We cannot dwell on the historical detail of it particularly, but let me mention verse 2 "Behold there shall stand up yet three kings in Persia". That came to pass; there did rise up three kings in Persia; Darius, Artaxerxes and Ahashuerus. These three kings stood up in Persia after the time of Daniel speaking. Then, verse 3 "And a mighty king shall stand up, that shall rule with great dominion and do according to his will", referring to Alexander the Great. Well, this happened exactly as it was said. Then, verse 5 "And the king of the South shall be strong; Alexander's kingdom was divided into four and the one who took the southern kingdom, Ptolemy waxed very very strong, just as God said. Then verse 6 "And in the end of years they shall join themselves together; for the king's daughter of the South shall come to the king of the North to make an agreement; but she shall not retain the power of the arm; "In those days the king of the South and the king of the North came together and the daughter of the king of the South, Bernice, married a son of the king of the North and so they formed a union, a federation of the two great nations. But it did not last and we read "But out of a branch of her roots shall one stand up in his estate which shall come with an army, and shall enter into the fortress of the king of the North". This young woman was discredited; she was set aside by the king of the North and so, later her brother, one out of the same roots as herself, rose up and sought to get vengeance for her.

Then if you look down to verse 13 "For the king of the North shall return, and shall set forth a multitude greater than the former". That king of the North is one called Antiochus the Great and all the details that are given to us here have been literally and historically fulfilled. Verse 17 "He shall also set his face to enter with the strength of his whole kingdom, and upright ones with him; thus shall he do: and he shall give him the daughter of women, corrupting her: but she shall not stand on his side, neither be for him". Here again, another woman comes on the scene, and she is the

CHAPTERS 10 - 12   145

famous queen, Cleopatra, of whom we have read in our childhood. She is called here the daughter of women because Queen Cleopatra was brought up by her mother and her grandmother. Then, verse 18, "After this shall he turn his face to the isles"; that was when he attacked Asia Minor, the isles, exactly as God had said. Verse 20 "Then shall stand up in his estate a raiser of taxes in the glory of the kingdom": Beloved, in those days there was a king, a son of Antiochus the Great, remembered in history to this very day as the raiser of taxes. Then, "And in his estate shall stand up a vile person", and that vile person is Antiochus Epiphanes, the Syrian emperor. Then we read, verse 29, "At the time appointed he shall return, and come toward the South; but it shall not be as the former, or as the latter". For the ships of Chittim shall come against him": now, the kingdom of Antiochus Epiphanes was destroyed by the ships of Chittim. The ships of Rome came against him and Antiochus was told to return and go back to his own kingdom: he asked for time to consider it and the Roman general drew a circle around him and said, "you must answer yes or no before you step out of that circle" and Antiochus, in shame, returned to his own kingdom and died an ignominious death. I have mentioned but one or two factors in verses 1 to 31 but if you care to go into it, if you look at a Bible dictionary or some other help, you will find that **everything** from verses 1 to 31 has been absolutely fulfilled as God said it would be.

But now we come to verse 32 and to what is yet future. Not now the conflict between Assyria and Egypt that has occupied us in the former verses but Assyria and Egypt together against the head of the revived Roman Empire. "And the king shall do according to his will; and he shall exalt himself, and magnify himself above every god". We saw earlier that this Roman monarch would arise and seek to exalt himself above all. Verse 38 "But in his estate shall he honour the god of forces; and a god whom his fathers knew not". He has been a Jew brought up to acknowledge the one

146 DANIEL

God. "Thus shall he do in the most strong holds with a strange god, whom he shall acknowledge and increase with glory: and he shall cause them to rule over many, and shall divide the land for gain. And at the time of the end shall the king of the South push at him: and the king of the North shall come against him like a whirlwind". Here are these two sworn enemies, these who were enemies for centuries: in the latter times, when the church is gone, banding together, and they will hurl themselves at the Roman emperor. "The king of the South shall come at him and the king of the North shall push at him". Now, from our earlier studies we noted that this Roman emperor would dominate the world and the whole world will be afraid of him. Now we are coming to the end of the seven years, and as they see the Man of Sin reeling under the plans of God, under the seals and the trumpets and the vials, these men take courage and realising the Man of Sin is weakening they rise up and attack him. They come from the North and the South hurling themselves at this Man of Sin, and he takes up the warfare. "He shall enter also into the glorious land, and many countries shall be overthrown but these shall escape out of his hand, even Edom and Moab, and the chief of the children of Ammon".

Now it is most remarkable, the Man of Sin comes to attack Israel and he rases the countries to the ground in his stride, but Moab and Edom and Ammon are spared: why is that? Because, when we come to Zechariah's prophecy we find that those countries are left for the judgment of Israel, it is Israel who judges these countries. Moab and Edom and Ammon were all related to Israel, descended from Israel's offspring. Ammon, you remember, was from Lot. Edom was from Esau and so on; they were all related by natural ties to Israel. If we turn to the book of the prophet Nahum, he says, "They regarded not the brotherly covenant; they broke their brotherly pledge with Israel and when Israel was being stricken, those nations Edom and Moab and Ammon stabbed Israel in the back and afflicted them in the time of

CHAPTERS 10 - 12   147

their great national calamity. Now God remembered that and so these nations are left for the judgment of Israel. They are spared the judgments of the Man of Sin to come under the judgment of Israel. "He shall stretch forth his hand also upon the countries: and the land of Egypt shall not escape. But he shall have power over the treasures of gold and silver, and over all the precious things of Egypt: and the Libyans and the Ethiopians shall be at his steps. But tidings out of the East and out of the North shall trouble him". Here we see the Man of Sin, this Roman emperor, hurling himself against the king of the North and the king of the South and he enters down into the land of Israel to attack them, but tidings out of the North and out of the East reach him. Tidings out of the North; that would probably be trouble in Russia; tidings out of the East, that would probably be China and Japan, what we call "the **yellow peril**". Well, as he hurls himself upon Israel tidings reach him and so he turns back again, God turns him back, and we read: "And he shall plant the tabernacles of his palace between the seas in the glorious holy mountain; yet he shall come to his end and none shall help him". Now beloved, here is the battle spoken of in the book of the Revelation chapter 16. The angel goes forth to gather the nations together to the battle of Armageddon. Israel (Palestine) has been the cockpit of the world, most of the great battles of the east have been waged in Israel because, as we saw earlier, it is a little buffer state between the mighty nations, Assyria to the North and Egypt to the South. Now at this time the king of the North and the king of the South are at war with Rome and the war is fought in Palestine, and there they are all together; the armies of these nations locked together in mortal struggle. And notice, they have got other nations confederated with them: Moab and Ammon and Edom are on the side of the king of the North and the king of the South, Libya and Cyrene and Ethiopia are on the side of the king of Egypt. The Beast has his ten kingdomed empire, and there the empires of the world are

148   DANIEL

locked in one deadly struggle, and just at that moment, as Palestine is being overwhelmed and the temple is destroyed and the land is desolate and the Jews have fled away through the Mount of Olives (where God has opened a way of escape for them): just at that crucial time, the Beast turns back with his armies; he hears of trouble, probably from Russia and from China, and right at that time the Lord appears, and we read: "And he shall come to his end and none shall help him". Right at that time the Lord appears for the rescue of His people (Israel). Though they slew God's Son, though they slew God's prophets, though they rejected God's word, though they turned away from God, yet the Lord appears to the rescue of His people. How does He come? Just as we see in Revelation 19, He comes back with His Church, the Church that was caught up seven years or more before that; He comes back with a two-edged sword out of His mouth and He smites the nations, and the Beast and the False Prophet are taken and they are cast into the lake of fire and Israel is delivered. Well, that is a very brief outline of the battle of Armageddon.

Finally, I want you to turn to chapter 12. In chapter 10 we saw the conflict in the heavens and in chapter 11 we have seen the conflict of nations. In chapter 12 we are going to see the conflict of God's people. In chapter 12, verses 1 to 4, we have the character of the end; then in verses 5 to 13 we have the times of the end. Verse 1 "At that time shall Michael stand up, the great prince which standeth for the children of thy people and there shall be a time of trouble, such as never was since there was a nation even to that same time: and at that time thy people shall be delivered, every one that shall be found written in the book". Now beloved, here is a description of the Great Tribulation. We have already mentioned about this time of tribulation. It is a remarkable fact that the Tribulation is only mentioned by name about four or five times in the Word; here in Daniel chapter 12;

CHAPTERS 10 - 12 149

Jeremiah 30; Matthew 24 and in Revelation chapter 3. In Jeremiah 30, Matthew 24 and here it is mentioned in connection with Israel. In Revelation chapter 3 it is mentioned concerning all the world, "to try them that dwell on the earth" says John. Despite these clear references some of God's dear people will bring the Church into it but God never mentions it in connection with the Church and it is never associated with the Church in the Scripture of truth. Mark you, I do not say that unkindly but I do want you to be established with me, grounded with me in the fact that our blessed Lord can appear at any moment. Brethren, I have seen christians losing the balance of their mind, christians having mental breakdowns by thinking that we have got to go through that dreadful Tribulation: thank God that we have got a hope better than that; a hope steadfast and sure that at any time we can expect our Lord from Heaven.

Well, now, here is the time of Great Tribulation "And at that time Michael stands up" Michael the archangel, looking after the nation of Israel, caring for the nation of Israel. "And at that time thy people shall be delivered every one that shall be found written in the book". During the time of tribulation there are two sections of Israel, the godly and the ungodly: the godly — those who receive the gospel of the kingdom and refuse to bear the mark of the Beast, the ungodly — those who bow to the Beast and worship his image. Now at the end of the tribulation they will be delivered: who? Those that are written in the book. Alas, two thirds of the Jews in Israel (Palestine) will perish in the judgment but one third, the godly third, will be preserved to come through the Tribulation and, they will be delivered, every one that is written in the book. Then the next verse "And many of them that sleep in the dust of the earth shall awake, some to everlasting life, and some to shame and everlasting contempt". Beloved, here is the national awakening of Israel, at the end of the Tribulation the nation

DANIEL

of Israel shall awaken out of the dust of the earth where they have lain for centuries, and Israel will become a nation indeed, but some of them shall enter into life and some into shame and everlasting contempt.

Then, verse 3 "And they that be wise shall shine as the brightness of the firmament; and they that turn many to righteousness as the stars for ever and ever". Oh, beloved, notice, in verse 1 we have the time of the end in relation to the godly remnant of Israel which will be delivered: in verse 2 we have the time of the end in relation to those who will be judged: in verse 3 we have the time of the end in relation to God's servants in that day, God's workers in the Tribulation who preach and Gospel of the kingdom and save many. Our Lord says that before He comes to reign the gospel of the kingdom will be preached among all nations and many shall turn to the Lord. So we find in Revelation 7 a multitude that no man can number out of every kindred and people and tongue and nation, saved after the Church has gone home. Let me repeat, of course, that they will not be people who have rejected the gospel in this present age but they will be people who have never heard the gospel. Children who had not reached an age of responsibility when the Lord came or heathen who had never heard the gospel. These will have an opportunity of embracing the gospel of the kingdom and being saved, and they will form the Lord's people on earth while the Church will be His people forever in heaven. Then, these workers, these servants of the Lord, who amid bloodshed and havoc have gone forth preaching the Word will shine as stars in the kingdom of the Father; they will shine as the brightness of the firmament and they shall shine as the stars for ever and ever.

Verse 4 "But thou, O Daniel, shut up these words, and seal the book, even to the time of the end: many shall run to and fro, and knowledge shall be increased". In verse 1 we saw how it affects the godly remnant of Israel; in verse 2 how it affects those that shall be judged; in verse 3 how it affects

CHAPTERS 10 - 12   151

God's servants. Now in verse 4 we find the effect of this on you and me. "But thou, O Daniel, shut up the words, and seal the book, even to the time of the end: many shall run to and fro and knowledge shall be increased". Daniel has been worried, cast down, has been in consternation, but he can just shut up the book, meditate upon it in his heart, dwell upon it in his soul and quietly rest in God, and know that many shall run to and fro and knowledge shall increase. Beloved we live in days when the germ of that, the seed of it, is being fulfilled; no doubt it will come to full fruition by and by but the germ of it is with us even now. "Many shall run to and fro; the word here used is a Hebrew word which means to go at a terrific speed, and men are doing it now. We read of aircraft that can fly at terrific speeds; we read of rockets that can fly even to the moon and planets beyond. The characteristic of the age is great speed. God says "many shall run to and fro" and it is coming true now but it will be more so after the Church has gone. But why are they running to and fro? It is the restlessness in the heart of men; a restless world that has rejected God's Son and so they are running to and fro on the earth. "And knowledge shall be increased." Ah! we see that now: God says men shall be heady and high minded, and we see knowledge increasing, and men of the world today have knowledge that our fathers and grandfathers never had: "knowledge shall be increased". Daniel "seal up the book", rest confidently in God. We know that the time is near and that any moment the Lord may come and take us to be with Himself.

Thus we have seen the character of the time of the end: now let us look at the times of the end. Verse 6, "How long shall it be to the end of these wonders?" and so the angel swears that there shall be a time, times, and half a time. Now, "a time" is a year, "times" are two years and "half a time" is half a year. The angel tells Daniel this is going to be fulfilled in time, times and a half". We are taken now to the middle of that week that we spoke about earlier and it is in the middle

DANIEL

of the week that the Man of Sin breaks the covenant — that is after three and a half years — time, times and half a time: a year, two years and half a year, three and a half years altogether. In $3\frac{1}{2}$ years from the time of the breaking of the covenant this shall be fulfilled. But then Daniel goes on and he says "And I heard, but I understood not: then said I, O my Lord, what shall be the end of these things?" And he said, "Go thy way, Daniel, for the words are closed up and sealed till the time of the end. Many shall be purified and made white and tried; but the wicked shall do wickedly: and none of the wicked shall understand; but the wise shall understand. And from the time that the daily sacrifice shall be taken away, and the abomination that maketh desolate set up, there shall be a thousand two hundred and ninety days".

Here again we come to this $3\frac{1}{2}$ years. Three and a half Hebrew years are one thousand, two hundred and sixty days, that is the period involved, but, with a little difference, as here it speaks not of one thousand, two hundred and sixty days, but one thousand, two hundred and ninety days. Thirty days more! why is that? Well, at the end of the Tribulation, when the Lord destroys the Beast and the False Prophet and the armies of evil, there will be a tremendous amount of wreckage, a tremendous havoc in the earth and so God adds these thirty days for the clearing up of the wreckage that shall be left after the Tribulation. Then, he goes on and he says "Blessed is he that waiteth, and cometh to the thousand, three hundred and five and thirty days". Now here is a bigger figure still. It is not one thousand, two hundred and ninety days but it is one thousand, three hundred and five and thirty days, what is that? Well, remember that after the Tribulation, certain things have to happen. There has got to be the first resurrection and the martyrs that were slain in the Tribulation have to be raised and there will be thrones set up, and then there has to be the judgment of the living nations, (the sheep and the goats have

CHAPTERS 10 - 12

to be separated). Then there is the gathering of the chaff from the wheat in the kingdom in Matthew 13. Now, all these things will take a little while longer and so, says Daniel "Blessed is he that cometh to the one thousand, three hundred and five and thirty days." This takes us beyond the first resurrection, beyond the judgments of the nations; right on to the time when everything is settled, everything accomplished and the Lord introduces the thousand years of millenial reign. Blessed are they that will enter into the Lord's kingdom on earth with all judgment behind them, and enter into the blessings of the millenial kingdom. But, oh child of God, just in passing, if it is blessed for those on earth, how much more blessed shall it be for you and me, who will be in heaven at this time, forever with the Lord! We do not appear here as Daniel is speaking solely of the earth, and, as the heavens are high above the earth, so much greater will be our blessing than the blessing of these wonderful people here. How gracious is our God! "But go thy way till the end be: for thou shalt rest, and stand in thy lot at the end of the days". Daniel was told to go his way for by and by he will rest, he would pass away, and rest in the presence of the Lord, but one day he will stand in his lot, his inheritance, at the end of the days. Well, that was Daniel's hope, that one day he would rest, he would die and pass into the place of comfort, into Abraham's bosom and by and by he would stand in his lot. But you and I have a hope far brighter than that; the scripture says "we shall not all sleep but we shall all be changed". Daniel knew he would sleep; you and I know that the scripture says that "we shall not all sleep but we shall all be changed" and so at any time our Lord may come, and if He came tonight you and I would not pass through the article of death but be changed and gathered up with the believers who had died and been raised, and, unlike Daniel, who will stand in his lot and will have a possession in the kingdom on earth, you and I will stand in heaven above, forever with the Lord, heirs of God and joint heirs with

Christ.

Now beloved, we have covered a large amount of scriptural territory in these final chapters but here again is the summary of it:—

Chapter 10 The conflict in the heavens.

Chapter 11 The conflict of the nations on earth.

Chapter 12 The conflict of the people of God.

Beloved, as we contemplate these things and we know the heavenly position of the Church in Christ let the cry go up from all of our hearts:

Even so come, Lord Jesus!